Thank you for your teaching.
Mar 23rd 1994.

KEEPING THE FAITH IN A CHANGING SOCIETY

For my parents

Martin A. Convey

Keeping the faith in a changing society

RELIGIOUS PRACTICE AND BELIEF IN IRELAND
IN THE LIGHT OF VATICAN II

the columba press

First edition published 1994 by
The Columba Press
93 The Rise, Mount Merrion, Blackrock, Co Dublin

Cover by Bill Bolger
Origination by The Columba Press
Printed in Ireland by
The Orchard Press, Dublin

ISBN 1 85607 092 1

Copyright © 1994, Martin A. Convey

Contents

Introduction   9

I: PRACTICE AND BELIEF: THE CONTEMPORARY IRISH CONTEXT

Religious practice and belief in Ireland since the Second Vatican Council   12
   The 'shallow belief' outlined by Michael Paul Gallagher (1974)
   The 'new type of Catholic' identified by Liam Ryan (1983)
   'Irish Catholicism is dying': Peadar Kirby (1984)
   Statistical analysis: Cause for concern

The Irish school context   22
   The Irish reliance on schools
   The 1976 primary school catechetical programme
   Catechesis in second level schools
   Syllabus for the religious education of catholic pupils in post primary schools (1982)
   Religion as an examination subject

Vocations in Ireland: a statistical analysis   34
   Attitudes towards vocations

Emergence of a renewed understanding of Christian ministry   36
   From clerical priesthood to communal Christian ministry

Conclusion   40

II: THE CATECHETICAL CONCERNS OF VATICAN II

Introduction   42
The search for a Uniform Catechism   44
   Local bishop as catechist vs. Universal Catechism
Catechesis and Vatican II: an initial overview   46
   Vatican II's Dogmatic Constitution on the Church
   Church as sacrament/sign
   Church as Pilgrim People of God
   Principle of collegiality
   Christian witness of The People of God

From pedagogy towards andragogy	55
From individual instruction towards communal formation	56
Return to the centrality of the liturgy	59
Vatican II's Constitution on the Liturgy	
The catechetical dimension of the liturgy	
Directives for the restoration of the adult catechumenate	65

III: THE FRUITS OF VATICAN II:
POSTCONCILIAR PERSPECTIVES ON FAITH DEVELOPMENT (1965-1972)

Introduction	69
The General Catechetical Directory	69
Background to the Catechetical Directory	
An overview of the Directory:	
Recognition of the present catechetical situation	
Catechesis: Part of the pastoral mission of the Church	
Adult catechesis as the chief form of catechesis	
The catechetical dimension of the liturgy	
Christ, the alpha and omega of catechesis	
The centrality of the Paschal Mystery	
Catechetical responsibilities of the Christian community	
Principle of adaptation	
The restored adult catechumenate	80
Vatican II's mandate for catechumenal restoration	
Structure of the R.C.I.A.	
Adult catechesis as communal journey towards conversion	
Initiation into the Paschal Mystery	
Overview of the R.C.I.A. :	85
The Precatechumenate	
The Catechumenate	
Period of Purification and Enlightenment	
Post-baptismal or Mystagogical catechesis	
Implicit communal ministries of the Rite	91
Implications of the Rite	92

IV: THE FRUITS OF VATICAN II:
POSTCONCILIAR PERSPECTIVES ON FAITH DEVELOPMENT (1973-1993)

Introduction	93
1977 Synod of Bishops on Catechesis	93
Concern for adult faith development	
Liturgical and communal dimensions of catechesis	
The content of catechesis	
Conclusions of the 1977 synod	

The 1983 Code of Canon Law 97
    Ministry of the Word
    Catechetical formation
    Sharing the responsibilities
    Missionary activity of the Church
    Catholic education

Paul VI and John Paul II: Uniformity and Divergence 107

Conclusion 113

V: FAITH DEVELOPMENT IN THE LIGHT OF VATICAN II: IRISH POLICY AND ACTION

Introduction 114

The present situation in adult education 114
    Attitudes towards adult education
    Participation in adult education courses
    Government policy on adult education

Adult catechesis in Ireland: The present status 122
    Early stages in the evolution of adult religious education
    Local community providing for adult religious education
    Church providing for adult religious education
    The basic needs of adult religious education emerge
    Contemporary adult religious education programmes
    From adult religious education to adult catechesis
    Towards a communal adult catechesis
    Wim Saris approach to catechesis at parish level: Ballinteer
    Towards a communal liturgical catechesis
    The 1972 Rite of Christian Initiation of Adults in action
    Where the future of adult catechesis lies

Awareness of the Irish hierarchy
to the necessity of adult catechesis 135

Conclusion 139

VI: KEEPING THE FAITH: PAST TRADITIONS, PRESENT SITUATIONS, FUTURE POSSIBILITIES

Introduction 141

The Tridentine legacy 141

Vatican II: Towards a new catechesis 144

Vatican II's Models of Church 146

The implicit model of Church in
    The Rite of Christian Initiation of Adults 150

Sacraments, sacramentality, initiation and formation 154

The parish and sacraments of adulthood	157
R.C.I.A. as model of sacramental initiation of minors	159
R.C.I.A. as model of adult Christian formation	161
Adult faith: The Irish context	163
The continued dependence on the Catholic schooling system	164
Keeping the faith: The way forward	165

GENERAL CONCLUSION

Conclusion 170

Notes 173
Glossary 191
Bibliography 195

Introduction

It is arguably true to say that, as far as Christianity is concerned, its greatest difficulties today have less to do with theology (reflection on, and formulation of, the faith) than with education (the introduction and initiation of new generations into a Christian value system and way of life). Such is evident from the increasing demands that are at present being made to re-examine the entire process of how faith is sustained and actively passed on from generation to generation. This is particularly true within the Roman Catholic Church where the issue of religious education (more recently referred to, within that tradition, as catechesis) has been debated at both Ecumenical Council and synodal levels in the recent past.

The Second Vatican Council [1962-1965], in proclaiming adult catechesis as the 'chief form of catechesis, towards which all other catechesis is directed', gave priority to both the religious and educational needs of the adult. This approach, which makes catechesis directed towards adults, normative, stands in marked contrast to the manner in which religious education was conducted prior to that Council. Here the usual setting for religious education was the classroom, the recipients children, and the chief method employed that of the question and answer catechism text. Such a change of emphasis marks a watershed in the history of religious education within the Roman Catholic Church.

The aim of this work is twofold: firstly, it attempts to offer a critique of religious practice and belief in contemporary Ireland and secondly, in an effort to discern how the Irish Church may benefit from Vatican II's insights and recommendations, it seeks to explore that Council's vision in relation to the theme of faith development.

Many of the conclusions and recommendations of Vatican II had, in fact, their roots deep in the practices of the early Church. This is particularly true in the case of its deliberations on catechesis when, during the first centuries of Christianity, catechesis directed towards adults was the norm. Since that time the catechetical system or model of Christian education has experienced a number of fundamental changes. These changes are relatively well defined and can be shown to have taken place within certain centuries.

In an earlier work I identified three such crucial changes to have occurred in the Christian educational endeavour as follows: during the fourth century (at the end of the era of the adult catechumenate – the first long-lasting educational model to have existed); during the eleventh century (at the beginning of a period of missionary zeal and evangelical preaching) and also during the sixteenth century (marked by the advent of the catechism – a product of the Reformation). A fourth model similar to the one utilised by the early Church was adopted by the Second Vatican Council – a model which sought, once again, to revert catechetical attention back to adults.

The first chapter of this work offers a critique of religious attitudes and practices in this country in the post-Vatican II era. It identifies a gradual (but marked) decline in formal Church affiliation and sacramental participation by some sections of the adult Irish population. Such trends are taken as indicative of the urgent need to provide for an appropriate catechesis – especially a catechesis directed towards the growing number of adults who are experiencing difficulty with their faith.

In an effort to discern why the Council recommended that adults should again become the primary focus for catechesis, the next three chapters examine the treatment of the theme of adult catechesis and faith development in the conciliar and post-conciliar Vatican documents. Here, particular attention is given to the post-conciliar *Rite of Christian Initiation of Adults* (R.C.I.A.) – the outcome of the council's mandatory recommendations to restore the adult catechumenate and afford primary attention to the faith development of adults.

In examining the actual development of, and resources presently given to, the process of adult faith development in Ireland, chapter V highlights a large inequality in favour of the primary and secondary school educational systems and, as such, indicates an immediate need to re-access the situation.

The final chapter relates the recommendations and insights of Vatican II to the contemporary Irish Church in an effort to discern how, in the future, it may benefit from them. One of the greatest challenges facing the Irish Church today is identified as that of coming to terms with the new educational model envisaged by Vatican II. This will involve a decisive movement away from the existing Tridentine model of Christian education as doctrinal transmission (with its structures and resources operating almost exclusively within the formal classroom setting) towards a model which holds Christian education as a multidimensional process of initiation into an adult Christian faith and way of life. To successfully achieve this aim the last chapter highlights the need within the Irish Church to draw upon the richness of, and implement fully, the refoms mandated by the council in relation to the associated areas of (adult) ministry and (adult) sacramentality. Finally, it is envisaged that the necessary way forward may lie in adapting the 1972 *Rite of Christian Initiation of Adults* to the Irish context and the possibility of such is explored.

Thirty years on, it is difficult to comprehend why Vatican II's preferred catechetical approach has not been discerned or fully analysed to date, nor why the implications of such an approach have not been explored by and for the contemporary Irish Church. This work attempts to assist in that task and, as such, should be of interest not only to catechists and theologians, but also to those involved in Christian ministry at any level. Indeed, the council's vision and understanding of Church and what being a Christian in today's world entails have, when brought to their logical conclusions, profound and significant theological and catechetical implications for all aspects of Christian living. This is especially true within the Irish Church where traditionally change comes about slowly and often with difficulty. If this work succeeds in initiating dialogue and debate on the existing system of Christian education and faith development in this country then it will have made a meaningful and valuable contribution. My hope is that it will.

Throughout the book the words 'religious studies', 'religious education', 'Christian education', 'Christian living', 'evangelisation', 'catechesis', 'adult religious education', 'Christian doctrine' etc. are used within specific contexts and with specific meanings. A glossary of such terms is included as an appendix.

CHAPTER I

Practice and belief:
THE CONTEMPORARY IRISH CONTEXT

RELIGIOUS PRACTICE AND BELIEF IN IRELAND SINCE THE SECOND VATICAN COUNCIL

Until the 1960s the Catholic Church in Ireland was largely at peace with itself. Full churches, a powerful and demanding authority structure, lack of any serious self-analysis or self-criticism, an enormously high profile in the so-called secular life of the people, control in the key areas of medicine and education – it was the 'Old' Church at its most expressive. The boat was steady in a sheltered harbour. The lapsing of some emigrants, the anti-clericalism of some writers, the occasional challenges from political life, none of these was serious enough to cause a storm. Rumours that Mass attendance was going down in Northern Italy or collapsing in other parts of Europe made little difference to us. The situation in Ireland was different. We could almost afford to be complacent.

And then the harbour wall came down. The boat began to rock under the influence of the wind and the waves. By the end of the 1960s Ireland was facing the open sea. Nothing was ever quite the same again. And there were some who breathed a deep sigh of relief.[1]

Such is the picture painted by one contemporary writer when outlining the rapid changes in Irish lifestyle that have taken place during the last three decades.

It is true that one has only to stroll through our larger towns and cities or drive through the countryside to realise the dramatic changes that have occurred in Irish society in the recent past. The Ireland of Kavanagh, Yeats, O'Casey and Joyce has been urbanised and industrialised. In the twenty year period 1965-1985 Dublin, for example, doubled its population to 1.5 million and became one of the most rapidly growing cities in Europe.

Like most Western societies, Ireland has experienced the positive and negative effects of the new age of technology. Unlike other

PRACTICE AND BELIEF: THE CONTEMPORARY IRISH CONTEXT   13

countries, the pace of change in Ireland in the immediate past has been more rapid and its effects more noticeable. Ireland has changed from a rural society of small close-knit communities to a modern technological society in a relatively short space of time. The effects of such change are still being felt in both the Church and society at large.

Apart from the *European Values Study Group* survey of 1981, the main concrete sources of information pertaining to the quality and depth of Christian faith in contemporary Ireland comes from the many surveys undertaken by the Research and Development Unit of the Irish Episcopal Conference. The major study here is the research on religious practice and belief in Ireland based on a random sample of 2,600 adults completed by Máire Nic Ghiolla Phádraig in 1975.[2] This has been supplemented by a study of Dublin adults by Micheál Mac Gréil (1974),[3] a study of adaption to religious values by university students by K. P. O'Doherty (1969),[4] a study of Irish university students by Thomas Inglis (1979),[5] a study of Dublin adolescents by Bernadette MacMahon (1981),[6] a survey of parochial life by Brigid Reynolds and Sean Healy (1983)[7] and a survey of senior school goers by Ann Breslin (1983).[8] The most recent study into the religious practice and values of Irish adults was conducted in 1990 by Micheál Mac Gréil.[9]

Influential theologians/sociologists/commentators like Michael Paul Gallagher, Liam Ryan and Peadar Kirby are some of the few who have also contributed to the discussion on the depth of Christian faith and belief in Irish society in modern times. Indeed, of the people who have written on the subject, all have outlined causes for concern. None have declared satisfaction with the present situation. The conclusions of Gallagher, Ryan and Kirby prove both interesting and challenging and merit separate treatment.

The 'shallow belief' outlined by Michael Paul Gallagher (1974)
One of the first to express deep concern about the level of faith of Irish adults was the Irish Jesuit priest Michael Paul Gallagher. His early writings are grounded mainly on his own pastoral experience working with young adults through the Department of English in University College, Dublin from 1967 to 1990. As early as 1974 he wrote

> What I have found is that the bottom has fallen out of conventional religion for many of those under thirty. What their parents believed and practiced sincerely as 'the faith' has turned

them off. What they were taught as religion in schools has gradually bored and even embittered them. What they experience for the most part in Church on Sunday is a dull ritual that does not express anything meaningful for them. The result [is] that their image of the Church and of faith is not something worth growing into. So they 'lose the faith' or perhaps more accurately, they lose hope that what is seen as 'the faith' could ever again come alive in their lives. [10]

Gallagher later identifies three reasons for this 'loss of hope': trouble in the teaching of religion in schools, failings in the pastoral ministry of the Church and weakness in the quality of Christian living in families and in Irish society at large. In an article written in 1978 he parallels the 'shallow ground' in the biblical Parable of the Sower to the failure of pastoral imagination within the Church itself.[11]

In relation to religious education in second level schools, Gallagher identifies the legacy the catechism has left behind in the Irish classroom:

> The teaching seems to have been geared more to correctness of doctrine and conformism of practice than to conversion of life and heart ... There still remain too many religious classrooms that are disaster areas for faith.[12]

Interestingly enough, Gallagher does not outline a solution to the problem solely in relation to students and teachers but rather suggests the necessity of a much broader approach: '... the main pastoral programme we need is not so much a dramatic apostolate for the young, themselves, but, through the schools, a real campaign of adult education for their parents, helping them to explore where they are in their own belief'.

In his more recent works, Gallagher's concern for the broader adult population (and not just for the young adults he came into contact with at university level) is further developed. He outlines his thesis that the greatest threat to Catholicism in Ireland is not 'unbelief' but rather 'shallow belief'.[13] 'Catholics,' he says, 'seem to be over-sacramentalised and under evangelised'. As a result the faith level of the adult population is not as deep as it could and should be. Three familiar words are used by him in relation to the present situation regarding adult faith: 'alienation', 'anger' and 'apathy'.

Perhaps it is these words which best sum up the evolution of the catechetical problems in Ireland in the recent past. Many adults in the sixties (immediately after Vatican II) did not understand, and thus felt alienated from, the 'New Church' which the council brought about. This, in turn, led to frustration and anger (particularly in relation to strict Church teachings on matters such as divorce and contraception in the seventies). That anger is today diffused into apathy. It is this apathy which is clearly identified in the works of Gallagher (and others) when writing on the topic of faith and belief in Ireland today.

As already mentioned, Gallagher's conclusions are based mainly on his own personal experiences of ministry and therefore it could be argued that they are, by and large, speculative as they lack statistical evidence. However, he does refer occasionlly to sociological surveys which seem to substantiate his claims. For example he mentions the findings of Bernadette McMahon, who studied the religious beliefs of a large number of Dublin teenagers.[14]

She discovered that most were unable to give an account of their faith. In spite of years of religious education at school, the majority of teenagers had only a limited conceptual knowledge of their beliefs. Their faith was shallow and immature and their image of God vague and unclear. Gallagher concluded:

> One is forced to the conclusion that more people are marginalised from the Church and faith internally, than their external behaviour would yet indicate. Full churches on Sunday may indeed be the opium of the clergy. If this is so, then one of the realities that has to be faced is the interior and hidden malnutrition of faith among the under-forties in the new Irish society of these [last] two decades.[15]

It is Gallagher's belief that the only kind of faith that will survive in modern Ireland is one based on a free personal decision. Inherited faith, which has never been personally appropriated, will quietly disappear, as it has already done in most European countries.

The 'new type of Catholic' identified by Liam Ryan (1983)

Professor Liam Ryan's contribution to the analysis of faith and practice in Ireland is based upon the conclusions drawn by him from the various surveys available to date. He reached similar conclusions to those of Gallagher. Ryan found Ireland still to be a pre-eminently religious country having a weekly Mass attendance of 90%, a monthly communion rate of 65%, a 95% belief in God's existence, a 95% belief in Christ and his Church as well as a 90% belief that Christ is present in the eucharist.[16]

However, on closer examination of the statistics Ryan discovered that:

> ... though nearly all believe in God, nearly a quarter are not sure about what sort of God this might be. Some 35% either reject or are not sure of a life after death. Nearly half do not believe in hell or the devil. Only 53% with third level education fully accept papal infallibility and over a third have difficulty with some aspect of Church teaching.[17]

Ryan correctly identifies a statistical distortion present in the available surveys because of the fact that conflicting values and beliefs are often held by the one person at the same time. There are, accordingly, three levels of values which must be identified and contrasted in interpreting the findings of religious surveys. They are firstly the 'Christian Ideal' of belief and practice (something towards which all should strive but which, in practice, is achieved by only a few), secondly the 'Pragmatic Ideology' (or personal value system which guides Christians in everyday life; it varies from person to person, but is for all a working compromise between the ideals of the Church and the demands of the world) and thirdly 'Actual Behaviour' of people (which usually reflects the second ideology but is expected to follow the first).

This explains why:

> ... it is noticeable that adherence to the Christian ideal is highest in areas of belief which have no great impact on people's everyday living: 92% accept the [dogma of the] Assumption of Our Lady; 94% believe in the Trinity of God. On the other hand, moral teachings of the Church such as the prohibition on divorce and contraception are accepted fully by only a minority of Catholics ... More significantly over one-third of the respondents report that religious principles seldom if ever guide their behaviour. This figure increases to 55% for city-born, and to 61% for the under-thirty age group. Over a third thought it right to put their own interests first and only 28% would put the demands of religion first if it clashed with the interests of family, work, or even recreation.[18]

Thus, like Gallagher, Ryan leads one to believe that a superficial adult Catholicism exists in contemporrary Ireland. He even suggests that the surveys point towards the emergence of:

> a new type of Catholic, as yet in a minority, ... characterised by an informed appreciation of the value of the supernatural and sacramental life of the Church, but retaining an independence of mind – largely on moral matters. The new Catholic demands that the Church speak more authoritatively and more often on matters of social morality but, at the same time, questions the Church's authority to speak on moral matters which affect his or her private life. Such Catholics are often liberal on sexual and marital questions but, at the same time, can be quite adamant about rejecting abortion.

These New Catholics

> ... continue to seek sacramental ministry from the Church at times when such ministry seems appropriate or necessary – for some, every day; for the majority every Sunday; for others, only at important feasts like Easter and Christmas or important occasions such as baptism, marriage or death. All want a more pastoral and less authoritarian style of Church leadership. Above all they like the newer theology which suggests that it is hard, rather than easy, for a reasonably religious person to commit a mortal sin.[19]

Ryan suggests that the central problem is that faith and religion have little impact on the daily lives of those who are practicing:

> It is clear that being a Catholic is not central to many people's lives. The pattern of Sunday Mass being an oasis in the overall pattern of life is quite marked. Religion appears as a self-contained compartment, adequate in itself, but divorced from the other compartments where the main activities of normal life take place. A picture emerges of a people largely believing in God and in the Church, but in posession of a belief which increasingly has little impact, not just on the wider world of business and politics, but also on many areas of private morality.[20]

'Irish Catholicism is dying': Peadar Kirby (1984).
Peadar Kirby, in his controversial 1984 study of the Irish Church, *Is Irish Catholicism Dying?*[21] outlines his personal thoughts on the state of the Catholic Church in Ireland.

Kirby's central thesis is that the Irish Catholic Church has failed to evolve a successful pastoral strategy to respond to the twin challenges of the last twenty five years – the economic and social reforms that have changed Ireland from a predominantly rural society to an urban one and also the violent renewal of the old conflict in Northern Ireland. This failure, allied to the subtly corrosive attacks of the consumer society on the Irish Catholic ethos, has resulted in a decline in the strength and depth of the Christian faith.

Kirby also criticises Church leaders for failing to fashion new structures to meet the needs of a new society. He contrasts the lack of vitality in the Irish Church to the enthusiastic development of the Church in Latin America and complains of the inability of Irish clergy to power-share with laity and involve them in pastoral ministry at parish level:

> There must be no other majority Church in any other country in the world which does not employ lay people to work in pastoral teams with priests and sisters, and to contribute their creativity in fashioning a whole variety of new Church structures to preach and embody the gospel effectively for the men and women of our time.[22]

He recommends a New Church for a New Ireland and subtitles his book *Liberating An Imprisoned Church*. According to Kirby, this New Church could learn from the models of Church emerging in the Third World, especially the basic Christian Communities of South America. Here people meet to reflect on their lives in the light of the scriptures and to pray together. They also see the struggle for justice as a gospel imperative. In this respect Kirby quotes from a 1984 article written by Niall O' Brien:

> Much prayer coupled with little justice guarantees atheism in the next generation.[23]

In criticising clericalism Kirby warns that if the Catholic Church in Ireland is to survive, it must become a Church of the people, especially the poor and marginalised. This will involve radical change and arouse much opposition, but the choice for Kirby is a simple one – change or die.

Kirby is especially critical of the leadership offered by the Irish Bishops in introducing to the Irish Church the changes mandated by Vatican II. He states that most bishops remained blind to the possibilities offered by the reforms of the Council. When finally introduced (out of necessity by virtue of allegiance to Rome) they were put in place in 'a Church which did not really feel the need for them'.[24]

With regard to catechesis, Kirby is very sceptical of the strategy of the Irish Church in relying so heavily on religious education in schools to give some Christian formation to young Catholics. Although many priests and bishops do their best to help develop an adult faith among their people, they do so through outmoded parish structures which more often hinder rather than help this process. Indeed, as the National Conference of Priests in Ireland stated at their 1981 annual meeting, 'Many priests do not have the vision of the Church central to Vatican II. There is little involvement of the laity, lack of team work in ministry, and a complacent acceptance of the status quo'.[25]

Interestingly enough, Kirby lists adult education for Christians as one of the seeds for a new model of Church which is just beginning to emerge. Such education would have its roots in a true local community. According to Kirby, the local parish, as it exists at present, does not mirror a true community precisely because of the lack of interaction and teamwork between laity and clergy.

It would be unwise to dismiss Kirby's observations on th' grounds of lack of substantiating evidence. When indepth surveys were undertaken the results confirmed much of his thoughts on the matter. I will now outline the major findings of these surveys.

Statistical analysis: Cause for concern
Sean Healy and Brigid Reynolds, in assessing religious practice and belief in 1985, drew attention to the following facts:[26]

* One fifth of the sample surveyed do not pray or draw strength or comfort from religion.

* One fifth have doubts about the soul, life and death and about heaven.

* One half do not believe in hell or the devil. (Here one commentator, Michael Fogarty, suggests that if the devil seems to walk freely in our world perhaps it's out of frustration at being ignored!).

* One half express less than 'a great deal of confidence' in 'the Church'.

* One half do not think 'their Church' adequately answers the problems of individuals or family life.

* Over a half no longer believe there is one true religion.

* 35% of the unemployed go to Church occasionally at best.

* Only 53% of those with third-level education fully accept papal infallability.

* Only 35% of those with third-level education believe divorce should not be allowed.

* Over one third state that religious principles seldom, if ever, guide their behaviour. This figure rises to 55% for city-born people and to 61% for those under 30.

* Only 28% would put the demands of religion above the interests of family, work or even recreation.

Interpreted as they are presented, the above statistics seem to outline a cause for concern. However, when examined in the light of Ryan's three levels of religious belief[27] it can be argued that it is unclear whether the statistics relate to actual behaviour or whether they represent a Christian Ideal, a Pragmatic Ideology or the personal value system of the individual. Obviously they do not represent the Christian Ideal of belief and practice which people strive towards. Thus, the statistics probably represent the Pragmatic Ideology of the individual.

However, the same surveys from which the above statistics are drawn reveal, by and large, that the actual behaviour of the people surveyed reflects more the Christian Ideal than their own personal beliefs and value systems – as the following statistics illustrate. In other words, the religious practice of Irish people proves to be more conservative than their opinions:[28]

* The Irish Church retains a popular loyalty to a degree unknown elsewhere in Europe.

* The tradition of Sunday worship remains strong even in the younger generation (some three quarters of Catholics in their twenties attend Mass weekly).

* Nearly 30 percent of people in the Republic go to Mass more frequently than weekly, and for reasons of personal conviction.

* The population prays frequently (over 80 per cent have some daily prayer).

* There is an inherited sense of Christian belonging in most families (and hence homes) that communicate faith.

PRACTICE AND BELIEF: THE CONTEMPORARY IRISH CONTEXT   21

* There is a weekly Mass attendance of 90 per cent.
* There is a monthly communion rate of 65 per cent.

Thus, religious practice of Irish adults is, by European standards, exceptionally high. However, Máire Nic Ghiolla Phádraig cautions that in Ireland 'unlike most countries, levels of belief are lower than levels of religious practice' thus suggesting certain social conformism.[29] The main cause for concern which the statistics unveil is among marginalised groups (particularly the unemployed, residents of built-up areas of large cities and those who have left school at a very early stage).

A more recent survey (conducted over the period November 1988 to April 1989) undertaken by Micheál MacGréil[30] reveals a new (but inevitable) aspect: religious belief has, in fact, now begun to affect religious practice as conformism diminishes.

Commenting initially on adult participation in Mass, communion and sacramental confession, MacGréil acknowledges that the study records a 'very positive level of liturgical and sacramental participation by the Roman Catholic adult population.'[31] Some 82% of the population attend Mass weekly and 63% receive Communion monthly.

The separate figures for Mass attendance indicate that the lowest levels of weekly participation are to be found in three adult groups: those aged between 21-35 years (71%), those reared in a large city (64%) and those who now reside in Dublin City and County (69%).

With regard to reception of Holy Communion, MacGréil again found that the same three groups received the sacrament less frequently than others of the sample. He draws attention to the fact that those with higher education tend to receive more frequently as do those with higher professional occuptions. For him such a situation merits 'pastoral analysis'.

Undoubtedly the greatest cause for concern highlighted in the report relates to sacramental confessions. 18% of those aged 21-35 never avail of the sacrament along with 19% of those with third level education. Again, the sacramental participation of those residing in larger cities indicates a cause for concern. Here 20% never receive the sacrament. The author comments:

> The practice of sacramental confession has been a strong characteristic of Irish Roman Catholicism. Its decline, therefore,

merits serious theological and pastoral examination and reflection.[32]

The most alarming aspects of the study are summarised on p. 20 of MacGréil's work. This table compares surveys relating to sacramental participation in Ireland (and, thus, formal involvement in the Church) over a fifteen year time span and, in doing so, answers the obvious criticism that to be of value, surveys must be compared to similiar ones conducted over a lengthy timespan. Here a 9% decline (in the space of fifteen years) in the practice of weekly Mass attendance is outlined. Even more alarming in this respect is the fact that the decline has accelerated in recent years. Undoubtedly, the greatest cause of all for concern lies in the area of sacramental confessions which witnessed an incredible drop of 29% (in those who availed of the sacrament monthly) over a fifteen year period.

MacGréil identifies the adults in question, who are withdrawing from sacramental participation, as being:

> ... young, middle-aged [21-35 year old] males, never married, city reared, Dublin dwellers, skilled and routine manual workers and those with incomplete second level education ...[33]

MacGréil does not suggest any reasons for the decline in sacramental participation. One can reasonably assume that the impact of a mostly materialistic way of life permeated through the media in all its forms has, among other factors, played a significant role. The next section will suggest that the Irish Church itself has not done enough in the area of adult catechesis to help those adults who have been shown to be most at risk of becoming alienated from formal sacramental participation. In short, the Church, through its inactivity, has contributed to the problem.

THE IRISH SCHOOL CONTEXT

Having outlined what can only be interpreted as a cause for concern to the Irish Church in relation to the recent emergence of a new lukewarm private Roman Catholicism, it is appropriate that the structures which nurtured such Catholicism be re-examined. As far as Ireland is concerned the main structures have been primary and second level schooling.

From the early nineteen seventies, many countries (especially North America) have shifted emphasis away from school oriented programmes of religious instruction towards a parish or community-centred programme.[34] However, large numbers of Catholic schools, especially on this side of the Atlantic, still attempt to provide an almost total 'catechesis' within the school system. This is particularly true in Ireland where, at present, there is increasing debate on the effectiveness of 'teaching religion' in school. One writer, for example, concluded:

> There are some things in religious education which they (schools) can do well. Others lie beyond their scope. It is important at present to define as clearly as possible what, religiously speaking, the school can reasonably be expected to achieve: beyond that we must mobilise the other educational potential of our Church, which is very considerable. We must try to involve the whole Church Community in the task of religious education.[35]

The Irish reliance on schools
If one examines the present educational structures in Ireland one can immediately see that the school has inherited, to a very large extent, the function of educating in faith. A number of factors which have brought about this situation can be identified. The first being the historical development of the National School System in Ireland which moved from a Protestant dominated system of educ-ation to a Roman Catholic denominational system. This came about because of the pressure exerted by the Catholic bishops in Ireland to ensure that Catholics would have an opportunity of receiving appropriate religious instruction. It was also supported by the rapid growth of religious orders whose main concern was proving education for the poor. Under many of these orders the school day centred on religious guidance and instruction.

Another factor was the concrete recognition by the State in the Constitution of 1937 that Catholic parents could enjoy the right to provide for the 'religious, moral, intellectual, physical and social education of their children', which effectively meant that parents could now send their children to Roman Catholic schools and so ensure they received instructions in the Catholic faith which these schools provided (a right which was not always granted to Irish parents over the centuries when subject to British rule). In recent years a decline in the religious practice of parents has increased the onus on schools to provide for the religious education of their pupils. So in the mind of many Irish parents, and indeed of teachers too, the primary (and, perhaps, sole) agent of catechesis today is in fact the school.

By and large, catechesis in Ireland is at present confined to school settings. Diocesan catechetical structures are devoted mainly to the support of their schools, notably political support, so that the Church can continue to enjoy the facility of teaching religion in State or State-financed schools. National catechetical structures deal with either programme content, production of teaching and learning materials, or teacher training.

One has only to examine the deployment of Irish diocesan priests even in the narrow area of second level education to gain an idea of how important the Irish Church views its involvement in the education of minors. Here, in one case, almost 20% of the diocesan priests working in a diocese are engaged in full-time second level education with 13.7% working in one school! However, the number of second level students in that diocese represents under 9% of the total diocesan population. To complicate matters even more, none of the priests concerned are employed as full-time catechists. The statistics reveal similar discrepancies in other Irish dioceses.

The contemporary setting is further compounded by the fact that dioceses in Ireland have never had to face the problem of large numbers of people (adults or children) totally unschooled in religion. In other countries, where such situations do exist, people have to be taught the rudiments of belief in out-of-school programmes. As a result, Irish parishes and dioceses have never developed a catechetical capability of any consequence. There seems to be no national structures intended to instigate or support parish catechetical programmes, or adult religious education. There is also a serious lack of involvement in catechesis at third level.[36] Without doubt, the over-reliance of the Catholic Church in Ireland on the primary and secondary schooling systems for the provision of a total and comprehensive catechesis ought to be re-examined.

However, the approach to religious education in schools today is very different from that of even ten or fifteen years ago. International research and development in the field of education have influenced the manner in which religion is now 'taught' – be it still almost exclusively at primary and secondary school levels. [37]

The shift which has taken place in religious education is due partly to the way in which Protestant scholars have approached the subject in the early part of this century. It was not until much later, in the 1940s and 1950s and more particularly in the light of Vatican II, that Roman Catholic scholars took a serious interest in the issue. Consistent with the newer approaches is the catechetical programme introduced into primary schools in 1976. This programme merits a general analysis as it provides a good example of the new insights in the field of catechesis already introduced at primary level.

The 1976 Primary School Catechetical Programme
This new programme, intended for use in primary schools in the whole of Ireland, was launched in 1976. The programme, entitled the *Children of God* series, incorporated many of the suggestions and recommendations contained in the post-conciliar *General Catechetical Directory*. It also drew from the findings in educational psychology and adopted recognised teaching strategies where they were thought appropriate.

In the introduction to the programme the authors outlined their catechetical approach. They state that:

> In this programme, religious education, or catechesis is understood as the communication of Christian revelation to children in their concrete situations with a view to fostering faith.[38]

Such an approach is, obviously, very different from the catechism method of religious education which preceded it. The catechism, as noted, was concerned chiefly with the communication of doctrine. The 'new' concern of catechesis is to foster a relationship with God and, as such, it must also be relevant to life and faithful to the content of the Christian message. In the words of the authors: 'the present programme seeks to take account of each of these concerns'. Conscious of the fact that faith must be relevant to life, the writers set out to 'explore with the children their experiences of the world and interpret them in the light of faith as a sign of the presence of God'.[39] The programme is, therefore, child-centred as opposed to the content-centred approach of the catechism which preceded it.

The child-centred approach has a social aspect as well as an educational one. This is consistent with the belief that catechesis and religious education must take place within the broader context of the community:

The parish, viewed as a faith community, also has an essential role in religious education. It provides the environment in which the effects of both parent and professional teacher can prosper.[40]

The effect of this approach is, therefore, to lead children to a 'deeper, more living, active and personal faith'.[41] Thus, adults in a community are very significant in the process of transmitting faith. This has long been borne out by the findings of sociological research. Sociologists have identified an educational model, which they call 'socialisation', based on the way societies incorporate new members.[42] This model has been applied to the process of catechising and is basic to the *Children of God* programme.

However, the information available on how successful the *Children of God* series is, and the attitudes of teachers towards its effectiveness, pose some awkward questions for the Irish Church. An impressive recent survey conducted by the Adviser for Religious Education in Primary Schools in the Archdiocese of Dublin concretises the suspicions held by many educators for a long time in the past. Desmond Murtagh sought, within the Archdiocese, to enquire into:

(a) the level of faith commitment of primary teachers who are expected to teach religion.

(b) their comfort with and willingness to teach religion.

(c) the support teachers experience in their work from parents and school chaplains.

(d) the level of use of the primary religious education programme.

Overall, the situation presents a positive picture with regard to teachers' faith, their willingness to teach religion and the support they receive from the school chaplain and the diocesan advisers. All of the teachers surveyed used the *Children of God* series and of them 76% expressed satisfaction with it.

Murtagh identified two areas of concern. The first being the percentage of teachers who would prefer not to have the responsibility of teaching religion if given the option. The second area of concern was identified as being the lack of parental support experienced by many teachers.[43]

The actual statistics revealed that for 21% of teachers, their own religious faith was perceived as being peripheral or irrelevant.

13% said that they attended Mass periodically or not at all. 24% said, if given a choice, they would not teach religion and 17% of respondents indicated that they have faith difficulties. 12% stated that, for them, teaching religion was either unimportant or just one more subject on the curriculum. The survey also revealed that 62% of teachers would like assistance from a trained catechist, while 22% would prefer to have a catechist 'teach' religion in their class.

Murtagh comments that the results of the survey give further support to those who question the effectiveness of the Church's role in school-based education, particularly in the area of handing on the faith.

Catechesis in second level schools
The perception and effectiveness of religious education at second level has, for some time now, been a source of concern for many educationalists and teachers.[44] Contemporary writers present an equally bleak picture of the present situation. Desmond Murtagh sums up:

> Schooling by its nature, is particularly well adapted to the transmission of cognitive content – facts, theories etc.. It is an effecient means of transmitting knowledge. However, the school on its own cannot transmit and nurture faith. The Church developed a schooling approach to religious education in an age when schooling could make explicit what children already lived implicitly within family life, parish participation and within the cultural environment. This partnership does not exist today but is too often presumed to exist.[45]

For him the way to overcome the situation is for the Church to provide adult/parent catechesis for those whom it claims to be the primary educators.

The results of Murtagh's localised study in the Dublin Archdiocese relating to primary catechesis are very similar to those of a recent national survey relating to second-level catechesis. The survey, *Whither Religious Education: A Survey of post-primary teachers in Ireland*, conducted in 1989 and published in 1991, is the first serious national survey to examine teachers' attitudes and observations relating catechesis at second level.[46]

Commissioned by the Episcopal Commission for Catechetics and the Catechetical Association of Ireland, the study found that 60 per cent of religious education teachers felt that teaching the subject was rewarding, but 38 per cent found it difficult. More than half (53 per cent) found some topics difficult, particularly theological issues, sexuality and the sacraments. A majority called for more resources to be given to religious education, for changes in the religious education programme and for the subject to be given exam status. Many believed religious education had a low status, particularly among junior pupils. The majority (69 per cent) felt religious education had a high profile among school administrators but its status was perceived to be lower among staff members (42 per cent), senior pupils (30 percent) and junior pupils (56 percent). One of the most interesting statistics related to the acknowledgement of more than 90 percent of teachers that, apart from schooling, they believed there were other effective ways of communicating the Christian message.

Perhaps the best insight as to how the leaders of the Church in Ireland, the Irish bishops, perceive religious education at second level can be gleaned from their 1982 Syllabus.

Syllabus for the religious education of Catholic pupils in post primary schools (1982)
The 1982 Syllabus was commissioned by the Irish Episcopal Commission for Catechetics, a body which has responsibility for schools' catechesis. The Syllabus is a brief document, twenty four pages in all, which, by its own admission[47] was written after the introduction of the catechetical programme for which it was intended.

Perhaps in recognising the inherent problem of preparing a fundamental document in the wake of secondary publications, the Syllabus cautions its readers that it should not be used rigidly, but adapted in consultation with the diocesan catechetical adviser.

The justification for the Syllabus is given as the need to evangelise each new generation within the Christian community. This process of evangelisation is served by various means, prominent amongst which is catechesis or religious education. Significantly these terms are used interchangeably throughout the document without distinction.

The Syllabus presents the general aim of catechesis (taken as it is from the *General Catechetical Directory*) to be primarily that of awakening people to an initial faith and, secondly, that of leading them to a mature faith. In the language of Gabriel Moran, religious education is concerned with the whole religious journey which parallels the human person's physical journey through life.

The Syllabus goes on to list ten further specific aims, subordinate to the general one. These can be classified under the combined headings of knowledge, understanding, attitudes and values. The aims are worth noting. According to the Syllabus, religious education should enable young people to:

1. become more aware of their own identity and worth as human beings created in the image of God.

2. deepen their relationship with God the Father, through the Son and in the Holy Spirit.

3. express their relationship with God in prayer and worship.

4. appreciate sacred scripture.

5. deepen their sense of belonging to the Church and encourage them to participate more fully in its liturgy and life.

6. deepen their understanding of the teaching of the Church and their awareness of its relevance to the questions, problems, aspirations and hopes of today's world.

7. develop a sense of mission to bring the truth of the gospel to the world.

8. develop a sense of solidarity with other people and a desire to put themselves at the service of humankind.

9. interpret the events and experiences of life in a Christian manner.

10. judge and act in accordance with the values of the gospel.

It is possible to interpret the above aims within the context of a conventional learning theory but to do so would be to underestimate the ultimate aim of catechesis which is a mature faith. If mature faith is taken to be the final end of religious development, then it could be compared to the end points of several models of moral and religious growth, i.e to Kohlberg's post conventional universal ethic stage; to Fowler's universalising stage of faith; to Moran's stage of detachment and to the stage of Revelation as described in Vatican II's constitution *Dei Verbum*.

Obviously, such ultimate end is typically associated with the later stages of adult life. Consequently it would be unrealistic to expect the school student to achieve it during adolescence. The Syllabus must, therefore, be interpreted with reference to the persons's whole life and not merely to the adolescent stage which is spent in conventional second level schooling – thus, the document indirectly points towards the necessity of life-long adult catechesis.

When one speaks in terms of personal faith development within a school context, the issue of assessment must arise. This will be dealt with in some detail later. Here it suffices to say that faith development, which pertains to the spiritual domain, cannot be readily quantified like the other areas of human development, since it is based on a personal relationship between the individual and his/her God. As far as the Syllabus is concerned the task of catechesis is to be shared between the home, the local community/parish and the school whose role has implicitly to do with the areas of knowledge and understanding.

'It is the whole Christian people who teach religion; teaches by the way it lives much more than by the way it lectures'.[48] Thus, the school is seen as a supplement to, rather than a substitute for the home and the role of the parents who are, 'he first religion teachers'. In this the Syllabus is echoing the Constitutional position which recognises the family as the 'primary educator of the child' In the absence of parental support, the school is seen to be inadequate in the total task of religious education, since Christianity is a way of life whose attitudes, values and practices are 'caught' from others, rather than 'taught'. [49]

The school, then, should inform and support parents, confirming them in their role rather than usurping that role from them. The local community or parish also has a major role to play in religious education. It is within the parish that the student will experience the liturgical and communal life of the Church. The school serves the parish by working in harmony with it and preparing and encouraging the student to participate fully in parish life. In terms of priority, the school is consistently listed as the junior partner in the trio of home, parish and school.

To describe the school as the junior partner is not to demean its status but merely to recognise the constraints under which it works. It is perceived as the provider of the knowledge and as the facilitator of understanding which enables the student to know what Christianity is so that he or she may then freely choose the Christian way. It should provide for religious education in two ways. Firstly, the ethos and curriculum of the school should be supportive of the process of religious education. The school should strive to create an 'environment of lived faith'.[50] The principal and staff are expected to work together towards the provision of this environment. The experience of school for the student should be that they recognise their dignity before they know its definition. Secondly, the subject religion should enjoy a level of status and treatment equal to other major subjects.

The document goes on to state that facilities and resources should be provided which are 'at least on a par with other major subjects'. The subject should be taught for a minimum of two hours per week, or three periods of forty minutes each. Teachers of the subject should be chosen on the basis of their commitment to the faith and their competence and willingness to undertake religious education. The teacher is identified as the primary resource who, by his or her own witness, gives authority to their teaching. In the words of the *General Catechetical Directory:* 'No text can take the place of a living communication of the Christian message'. Consequently the teacher should be adequately trained and supported with ongoing education and training. Such support should also include financial assistance where necessary. Attention should be given to prayer, liturgy and retreats and regular provision ought to be made for these activities.

Overall, the Syllabus emphasises the fact that process is equally as important as content: 'What is taught is not more important than, or independent of, how it is taught'.[51]

On the one hand, the Syllabus is prophetic in its statement of the vision for religious education. On the other hand, it is simply realistic in its plea for minimum standards – parity, at least, for the subject of religion with other subjects within the overall curriculum. The latter are examinable at national level in state exams; the former is not. This distinction should help to make the subject of religion an enclave of sanctity in an otherwise pressured and exam-oriented curriculum. In practice, it reduces the status of religion and raises the question of the credibility of the subject as has already been documented by several practising teachers: Casey,[52] Ní Mháille,[53] and Hanna.[54]

Gabriel Moran once suggested that the Catholic Church should run not Catholic schools, but good schools. The fact that Church-managed schools are being drawn inexorably towards increased State control, the result of State funding may compel the realisation of Moran's suggestion. The burden of catechesis will therefore rest increasingly on the parish/community and on the family and home. This ought to lead to a broader questioning of the practicality of the aims of the Syllabus with regard to the school.

Religion as an examination subject
The question of formal assessment at Leaving Certificate level has, for the moment, been placed in abeyance. The introduction of religion as an examination subject is not a panacea for the ills of the current religious education programme, as pointed out by a report issued jointly by the Catechetical Association of Ireland and the Diocesan Advisers of Religious Education in postprimary schools.[55] Such an assessment would create its own problems, most notably the narrowing of the programme to an academic/content focus to the exclusion of the affective, student-centred aspects of the course.

The whole question of the possibility of introducing Religion into the Irish Secondary School Curriculum as an examination subject is one which evokes much division in catechetical thinking. Many see such a possible introduction as an event which would offer a solution to the current problems already outlined. Others see such an introduction as, at best, meaningless and, at worst, harmful to faith development in youth.[56]

The policy of the Irish Episcopal Commission on the matter seems quite clear. As far back as February 16th 1977, a formal application was made on their behalf to the Department of Education requesting that Religious Studies be introduced as an examination subject at pass and honours level in the Leaving Certificate examination. The reasons given were as follows:

(a) Religious Studies is of unique importance as an academic discipline since it is the presentation and study in depth of the faith of a believing community. Its special requirements have been acknowledged in the legislation of other countries and in universities throughout the world for centuries.

(b) It appears likely that theology will be a subject in at least some of the Irish Universities in the near future. Preparatory provision for following such a course should be provided in the secondary school.

(c) All Roman Catholic students study religion throughout their secondary course. Those who develop a special interest in Religious Studies should be allowed to present it, as they would any other subject, in their final examination and should be awarded a certificate of competence if they reach a satisfactory level.[57]

The three reasons outlined above offer a significant indication of the Irish Episcopal Education Commission's understanding of the existing catechetical situation in second level schools and of their underlining philosophical assumptions in this field.

On their own, the reasons offered appear weak and certainly not consistent with Vatican II's approach to catechesis. Firstly, the unique importance of Religious Studies as an academic discipline in the study of the faith of a believing community represents more a return to the content approach of the past (in the form of the catechism) than a step in the future towards a community-centred methodological approach. The legislation of other countries pertaining to its status in the universities is, in many cases, a product of the Reformation where Chairs of Theology were established by the state to promote the reformed state religion. Such a reasoning today is both philosophically and educationally unsound as it does not facilitate authentic non-confessional education.

Secondly, the possible introduction or non-introduction of theology into the universities is largely irrelevant – at the moment three universities in Ireland offer courses in theology. Philosophy, anthropology and sociology, like theology, are very popular university subjects – but are not included in the secondary curriculum.

The third reason – that students are entitled to Leaving Certificate recognition of their competence – is seriously open to question. If catechesis is understood in the light of Vatican II as the 'in depth presentation and the study of the faith of a believing community' then it would appear that it ought to be the believing community and not the state which ought to give proficiency in it due recognition. Only a type of Religious Studies which would be from 'outside the believing community' and which could be taken up equally by students of any denomination can be appropriately crowned by a state-awarded certificate of competence.

A Draft Syllabus accompanied the application of the Episcopal Commission on Education to the Department of Education outlining what it considered ought to be included and suggesting three hours class contact per week. On this matter one teacher was tempted to wonder about 'how many years of practical classroom experience went into drafting the Syllabus'.[58]

Perhaps the most disturbing feature of the new syllabus among Leaving Certificate examination subjects is that it marks a departure from the separate idea of catechesis in the school – a strange move to take in the year when catechesis was the topic for discussion at the Roman Synod of Bishops. Catechetics, it is generally recognised, is a pastoral activity. The main aim of the catechetical teacher is the Christian development of the pupil – not their academic proficiency. Admittedly, school catechesis should provide a reasoned-out framework for it and make use of reason to work out the implications and the applications to the faith. But the emphasis ought to be pastoral and the strictly academic or scientific dimension of religion must be presented in a pastoral context.

A state examination and a certificate of 'competence' do not fit into such a context. Christian Doctrine – to employ the old term – can only be taught to students who already have a certain level of faith and who wish to grow in it or, exceptionally, to students who are willing to be led to faith. The weakening of the Christian environment and the corresponding weakening of the implicit social educational dimension seems not to have been taken into account. In short, the communal dimension of catechesis in the midst of an adult faith community does not receive any consideration.

Having outlined above some of the weaknesses and problems facing contemporary Irish Catholicism as well as the obvious inability of the Catholic school system to provide a 'total' catechesis, the final section of this chapter will explore another problem area – that of religious vocations. Here the chief aim will be to suggest how and why the existing Irish Church faces ever increasing difficulties in maintaining the present status quo in the system.

VOCATIONS IN IRELAND: A STATISTICAL ANALYSIS

Most of the statistics relating to vocations in Ireland have been widely published and, thus, are readily available. The statistics indicate that in the period prior to Vatican II the number of priests ordained each year showed signs of a slight downward trend.

The situation in the post-conciliar era proves less healthy. Over the last twenty years there has been a dramatic drop in the number of vocations to the priesthood and religious life in Ireland. This drop has been steepest in the case of religious orders and men choosing to minister abroad. The overall decline in the number of diocesan priests in Ireland during the same period has not been as great. John Weafer presents figures to show that the total number of diocesan priests in Ireland in 1988 is just 3% below the number in the country in 1970 (3,697 as opposed to 3,813). However, there was a 31% decline in the number of religious priests over the same period (2,789 as opposed to 4,019).[59]

In 1986 the Council for Research and Development projected that by 1996 there will be a further decrease of 4% (164) in the number of diocesan priests in the country. That projection is based on an estimate that 24% of the priests then alive in 1986 will have died by 1996 and on the assumption that an average of 71 men will be ordained each year for Irish dioceses (The average number of ordinations for Irish dioceses in the period 1978-1987 was 75). On the other hand, the Research and Development projection for the number of religious priests in the country by 1996 indicate that there will be a further 32% drop in this group. I will now examine in brief the possible reasons for such a decline, beginning with an analysis of attitudes towards vocations in contemporary Irish society.

Attitudes towards vocations
It is commonly believed that vocations to the priesthood and religious life have declined rapidly in recent years due, among other factors, to the 'increasing affluence and urbanisation of an extending industrial civilisation' – in short, secularism. It is also commonly believed that, by and large, Irish society today does not encourage or foster vocations. However, social scientists lead one to believe otherwise.

The 1972 survey commissioned by the Irish hierarchy on *Attitudes of Young People Towards Vocations* and carried out by Newman, Ryan and Ward in conjunction with the Research and Development Unit of the Catholic Communications Institute, do not indicate discouragement or antagonism towards vocations.[60] The situation does not seem to have changed significantly in the meantime. Mac Gréil, in his 1991 work, notes that:

> there is a very positive disposition towards vocations to the priesthood ... The very low percentage of respondents who would discourage a son or daughter from becoming a priest or a nun hardly substantiates the view that there is a serious domestic hostility to vocations.[61]

EMERGENCE OF A RENEWED UNDERSTANDING OF CHRISTIAN MINISTRY

The task of interpreting why such a dichotomy exists between the apparent sustained level of encouragement and fostering of vocations on the one hand and the rapid decline in the actual numbers entering seminaries and houses of formation on the other (the task of, as it were, putting flesh on statistical bones) is a difficult one. I suggest it may have much to do with the emergence of a renewed model of ministry in the Church since Vatican II. The advent of feminism has, for example, been one issue which has made many people (both women and men) aware that ministry within the Christian community is not something reserved to the ranks of the ordained but that by virtue of one's baptism, with few exceptions, a person is able to carry out many of the duties once thought to be the sole prerogative of the priest. The recognition of a universal priesthood of the baptised makes this possible.[62]

Thus, it can be argued that a renewed theology of ministry may have contributed to a decline in vocations since ministry is beginning to be understood again, as it was in the early Church, as being community-centred and community-structured. Consequently 'serving God' in the Christian community does not, by any means, necessarily entail sacramental ordination.

Michael Warren, when writing on the subject of ministry and catechesis in Ireland, was quick to draw similar conclusions. He recalls meeting a youth who had left the seminary in Maynooth and who was hoping to finish his theological studies. Warren recalls how the student outlined the dilemma in which he found himself:

> If I went to my bishop and told him that I thought I might have a vocation to be a priest and that I was willing to begin studies for the priesthood, I would get every kind of openhanded encouragement. If I didn't have the means, I would receive financial help ... However, if I went to my bishop and told him that I had been in the Young Christian Students and Young Christian Workers since I was fifteen, and that I had been spending almost twenty hours a week working to develop a Christian understanding among the unemployed in Dublin, and that I was finishing a degree in religion in St Patrick's College and wanted to undertake a full-time ministry with young people in the Church, I would receive the bishop's good wishes and no more.[63]

Commenting on the declining numbers of vocations to the ordained priesthood, Bishop Laurence Ryan drew attention to the fact that this situation would result in the Irish Church seeing ministry in a new light: 'Ministry in the Church is much wider than the ordained priesthood. The extent to which lay people exercise – or are encouraged or allowed to exercise – the many areas of ministry which are theirs by virtue of their baptism has an obvious bearing on the numbers of priests which are needed'.[64]

Ryan sees the pastoral task ahead which faces bishops, priests and laity in this country as being to 'prepare people for collaborative and team ministries'. This understanding of ministry is not new but rather it marks a return to a New Testament model of Christian ministry which merits a brief review.

From clerical priesthood to communal Christian ministry
In the entire history of the Church it is possible to outline at least four significant changes in an evolving pattern of priestly ministry, each with its corresponding theology of priesthood. Although such changes are mainly concerned with issues which are of a strictly theological nature, they are of significance to the present study for several reasons. Firstly, changes in the understanding of priesthood/ministry have implications in the entire field of catechetics. Secondly, these changes offer some insights into the large fall-off in vocations in recent years. Thirdly, the changes are, in fact, linked to the major catechetical changes which occurred in the history of the Church. Lastly, they have valuable contributions to make in identifying where the future of adult catechesis/faith formation lies.

For these reasons a brief account of the evolution of the contemporary understanding of priesthood and ministry is important. While such an account indicates that many of the current theological debates on the subject have deep roots in unresolved issues of past history, its chief aim is to open the debate on catechesis as a ministry directed to, and centred in, the entire adult Christian Community.

The changes can be outlined as follows:[65]

(i). The shift from an Old Testament model of priesthood to a New Testament one.

In ancient Israel the Levitical priesthood comprised of an elite caste; admission was strictly on the score of ancestry. The Hebrew priest functioned primarily as a man of the sanctuary. With the emergence of the Rabbi the priestly caste was practically confined to the conduct of cult. It is important to note that Jesus did not belong to the tribe of Levi and never actually refers to himself as a priest of that kind. Within the Judaism of his day Jesus would have been ranked a 'layman' as he did not join the same clerical elite set apart from the people. The only New Testament reference to Christ as 'priest' appears in the Letter to the Hebrews, where the author sees Christ as the perfect mediator between God and humankind and who, by his incarnation, death and resurrection, put an end forever to the need for a Levitical priesthood.

The New Testament does not understand the leaders of the apostolic Church as Levitical priests of the New Covenant. Early Christian community leaders are never called 'priests' and the Church continued to avoid usage of the term lest they be confused with the role of the Jewish and pagan priests. What does, in fact, emerge is a community of disciples and within that community a variety of charisms and ministries. Those who exercised such charisms and ministries understood themselves as part of the community – not as a separate class removed from it.

(ii). The shift from a New Testament model of priesthood to a sacerdotalist and hierarchical understanding.

Over the centuries, particularly with the Church's changed political status under Constantine in the fourth century, the ministry of leadership in the Church came to be patterned more and more on the style of Levitical priesthood with the emergence of a 'clerical' dimension. This was facilitated by the collapse of The Roman Empire and the taking over of secular roles of importance by local Church leaders.

As the Church moved into the middle ages there seemed little awareness of the New Testament conviction that all the baptised share in the universal priesthood of Christ and the mission of the Church, or that the Holy Spirit enriches the Christian community with various ministries for the fulfilment of its mission. There was an inevitable decline in the significance attached to non-ordained ministries. From this time onwards it is no longer baptism but Holy Orders which enables one to 'minister' in the Church. Significantly, ministry for the priest became confined to administering (as opposed to celebrating) sacraments to and for (as opposed to as part of and within) a Christian community.

(iii). The shift from a medieval understanding of priesthood to the controversies of the Reformation.

With the advent of the Protestant Reformation, reformers like Calvin and Luther laid down the main lines for a Protestant understanding of ministry, playing down the difference between the priesthood of the ordained and that of the baptised. The preaching of the gospel was to be the heart of Christian ministry as opposed to re-enacting the sacrifice of the eucharist (which, in fact, they did not attribute to this 'ritual'). The Council of Trent, for its part, did not seek to embark on a revised theology of priesthood. Instead it sought to defend the existing one. Thus, the difference between the priesthood of the ordained and that of the baptised was strongly reaffirmed.

(iv). The shift from a polemical theology of priesthood ('a theology against the Protestants') to a broader ecumenical understanding of priesthood at Vatican II.

Despite the great endeavour of the council to situate ministry not above the Church but within it, one is still left with some difficult theological questions – as can be noted in several of the documents of the council where two different theologies of priesthood compete for attention.

The late patristic age and the early middle ages leaned towards portraying priests and bishops as a kind of Christian version of the Old Testament Levitical priesthood. This interpretation is not entirely absent in Trent's theology of priestly ministry.

Vatican II acknowledged this imbalance and sought to return to a richer New Testament understanding. Yet the idiom of a later Tridentine development keeps reappearing, as when a council text chooses to refer to the dignity of the bishop in terms of a 'high priesthood' (*cf Lumen Gentium*, 21), a language undoubtedly reminiscent of the Levitical priesthood.

It is understandable that Vatican II was reluctant to abandon this kind of language, especially since it offered a ready means of defending the unique priesthood of the ordained. But it still leaves two divergent theologies of priesthood side by side in the documents of the council.

Such ambivalence is also to be found in the documents which have come from Rome since the close of the council. A good example is the revised 1983 *Code of Canon Law*. Here, on the one hand, it speaks in 'hierarchical' language about priesthood and at the same time invites the laity to 'equality' and 'participation'. Canon 208 reads:

> Flowing from their rebirth in Christ, there is a genuine equality of dignity and action among all of Christ's faithful. Because of this equality they all contribute, each according to his or her own condition and office, to the building up of the Body of Christ.

The canon immediately prior to this one (Canon 207) states:

> By Divine institution, among Christ's faithful there are in the Church sacred ministers, who in law are also called clerics; the others are called lay people.

Collectively the two canons can give the impression that the greatly larger group consisting of the laity are in no way of 'divine institution' and that their ministry cannot be considered 'sacred'.

Much more research is required in this area of theology. For the moment it will suffice to state the Roman view that by ordination to the priesthood a man is entrusted with a ministry through which he acts in the name of Christ the head, a ministry which does not come from within the community of the faithful or belong to that community from baptism. Thus, there is a clear distinction between the universal priesthood of the baptised (in which all share by virtue of their sacramental initiation into the Church) and the priesthood of the presbyterate (in which only those chosen by Christ may accept to share in).

The contemporary problem, as far as catechesis is concerned, lies less with the dichotomy between the priesthood of the baptised and that of the ordained than with the association of different ministries to each group.

CONCLUSION

This chapter has indicated that Irish religious belief and practice has changed significantly since Vatican II. The change has mainly been associated with a fall off in numbers receiving the sacraments (and, by implication, of affiliation to their Church). There are also indications of a 'new kind of Catholicism' emerging – a Catholicism which has become private, compartmentalised and divorced from everyday living.

The lack of implementation of the catechetical insights of Vatican II within the Irish Church has contributed greatly to this situation. In remaining entrenched in a system which succeeded well in vastly different circumstances in the past, Ireland is today particularly guilty of too great a reliance on a Catholic school system to educate minors in faith.

The fact that vocations to the religious life and priesthood have declined rapidly in this country, would seem to indicate that there are serious problems with superficial parish faith communities and/or with the manner in which present religious and priests see and exercise Christian ministry. In this respect it has been suggested that catechesis ought to be understood as a communal ministry (one of many) in which all have obligations to participate.

CHAPTER II

The catechetical concerns of Vatican II

INTRODUCTION

Having outlined many of the problems associated with religious practice and belief in contemporary Ireland, it is now appropriate that one examines the recommendations offered by Vatican II on how to maintain and pass on Christian faith in (what was even in the sixties) a rapidly changing society.

Such a task, however arduous, is essential. Without an adequate knowledge of the important insights of that Council in this area it is not possible to solve (or even discern) the weaknesses of Irish Catholicism alluded to in the previous chapter. Similarly, without a vision of what contemporary Christian faith ought to entail it is impossible to assess the faith as it presently exists. Thus, in asking how best Christianity is to be passed on to new generations, the next three chapters explore the thinking of the Fathers of Vatican II on the essence of Christian faith and the methods of its transmission. These two key areas are central to the science of catechesis. Thus, we will explore the catechetical concerns of Vatican II.

The concept of catechesis, itself, tended to be viewed within a post-Tridentine shadow right up to the eve of Vatican II. It had become content-centred in so far as it became widely understood in the narrow sense of handing on the established traditional truths of the Church in time-hallowed formulae. This approach was due almost entirely to the emergence of the catechism as a powerful and unique catechetical tool. However, it was precisely this approach which Pope John XXIII laid open to question from the very beginning in his opening address of the Second Vatican Council when he drew attention to the distinction between truth (the faith) and the manner in which it is expressed (the catechism):

> ... the authentic doctrine ... should be studied and expounded through the methods of research and through the literary forms of modern thought. The substance of the ancient deposit of faith is one thing and the way in which it is presented is an-

other. And it is the latter which must be taken into great consideration, with patience if necessary... [1]

To speak, then, of a catechesis in the spirit of Vatican II, is not to ask for a final re-statement in different terminology of the traditional doctrinal and moral statements – the unchanging deposit of faith. Rather, it is to seek a vision of the Church's understanding of itself and of its mission to the world.

The main concerns of this council were thus, as expected, with the concepts of Church, divine revelation, liturgy, ecumenism and mission as expressed through its sixteen documents. These documents do not (and were not intended to) end discussion on various questions for all times. Rather they provide the starting point for important advances. However, our immediate concern is not the history of Vatican II, nor a theological reflection on its documents. Rather, our chief aim is to examine the council's new vision of the Church and its mission face to face with the contemporary world and secondly to highlight the catechetical implications implicit in such a vision. Knowledge of the Church's understanding of itself and its mission is indeed critical because it is this understanding which will determine the content and appropriate methods of catechesis.

We begin with the council's deliberations on the question of the importance of the catechism as a catechetical method – an area which had been a major point of contention from the beginning of this century. Next the council's vision of the Church and her mission will be examined. I identify five major methodological changes for catechesis implicit in this 'new' vision. These will be analysed separately. They are:
a) The emergence of the notion of collegiality.
b) A renewed understanding of the value of Christian witness.
c) A movement from pedagogy towards andragogy.
d) A movement from individual instruction towards communal formation, and finally
e) A return to an understanding of the liturgy as a primary catechetical source.

The final section of this chapter will deal with the crucial call of the council to re-establish the adult catechumenate, thus paving the way for the centrality of adult catechesis which would be more concretely expressed later in the post-conciliar documents.

THE SEARCH FOR A UNIFORM CATECHISM

The question of the effectiveness of the catechism as a primary method of religious education was one which was brought up at the very beginning of the council. An examination of the preparatory documentation for Vatican II reveals numerous suggestions favouring uniformity in religious education.[2] A few bishops, attuned to the movements for renewal (both liturgical and catechetical) already underway in the Church, made recommendations that showed they were at least aware of the signs of the times. Yet twenty-two specific requests were put forward for a single catechism for the entire Church. Many other recommendations implicitly favoured such a religion text. Perhaps more interestingly still, there was a recommendation for a master text, or codification of basic teachings. The proposals from the Catholic Universities didn't mirror any great sensitivity to updating Catholic religious education either, except from some pastoral observations from Rome's Gregorian University.

In the light of later developments perhaps the most insightful recommendation turned out to be that of Bishop Pierre-Marie Lacointe of Beauvais in France. He advocated that instead of a universal catechism, as Vatican I had envisaged, it would be much more beneficial to the Church to have what he termed a *Directorium* – catechetical guidelines adopted to different groups in different cultures.[3] Viewed against the prevailing outlook, Lacointe's suggestion made him appear as one of the very few bishops who understood fully the limitations of the catechism approach to catechesis. Lacointe sent his suggestion (as did most other bishops) to the preparatory commission in 1959. Some twelve years later the *Directorium* became a reality. This directory will receive a more exhaustive treatment in the next chapter.

When the Council opened on October 11, 1962, the agenda included a *schema* on the 'Care of Souls'. One chapter of this document dealt with catechesis. The much-touted proposal for a uniform catechism was officially abandoned and in its stead the new *schema* advocated a set of guidelines or a 'directory' to serve as a basis for various national directories. The bishops never got around to discussing this. The topic failed to get out of committee stage because of the myriad redrafting of other council documents. Ultimately the chapter on catechesis was whittled down to a recommendation in the final document on the Office of Bishops which called

THE CATECHETICAL CONCERNS OF VATICAN II   45

for the preparation of a Catechetical Directory.[4] Not until the first Synod of Bishops gathered in Rome in 1977 was this recommendation back in the public arena once again. [5]

It would be inaccurate to suggest that the council paid little attention to the area of catechesis. In fact, it did but it realised that a catechetical model is based upon a certain understanding of Church, sacraments, ministry etc. It was towards these 'basics', then, that the fathers of Vatican II first turned their attention, choosing largely to leave the catechetical implications unexplored until immediately after the Council.

Local bishop as catechist vs universal catechism
In general, Vatican II returned to the catechetical methodology of the early Church and, in several of its major documents, highlighted the responsibility of bishops in preaching and teaching (as opposed to the faithful learning from the catechism). For example:

> ... the bishop should be first and foremost a herald of the faith, leading new disciples to Christ.[6]

and:

> In exercising their duty of teaching, they should announce the gospel of Christ to men, a task which is eminent among the chief duties of bishops.[7]

and again:

> It devolves on sacred bishops, who have the apostolic teaching, to give the faithful entrusted to them suitable instruction in the right use of the divine books, especially the New Testament and above all the gospels ...[8]

Ironically, however, another attempt was made to rehabilitate the goal of a uniform catechism. A report, drawn up in Rome, advocated a moratorium on new catechisms and the compilation of a model text to which all future catechisms should conform.[9] The point was made that, since the Council of Trent had come up with its catechism for pastors and Vatican I with its decree on a single catechism, Vatican II should have generated a similar project. The report, having made a case for the catechism, then proposed that it be executed by a future synod. This decision must, however, be interpreted against the background of the widespread controversy which then raged over the so-called Dutch Catechism; a new catechetical handbook for adults recommended by the Dutch hierarchy which contained, in the opinion of many theologians, unorthodox teaching.

Cardinal Jean Villot was one of the first bishops who chose to directly address the question of a catechetical directory. What he envisaged was a book of guidelines, the implementation of which would be optional for individual bishops; not a set of laws which would be universally mandatory. This directory, he affirmed, would be a sign of collegiality and would not usurp the compilation of individual catechisms by the various conferences of bishops. Since the project was destined for use by bishops' conferences throughout the world as they saw fit, the role of the Roman Curial Congregation in its compilation shifted from that of legislator to counsellor. That shift of emphasis closed one chapter in the history of catechesis which dealt with the debate of content versus method – at least in the short term.

CATECHESIS AND VATICAN II: AN INITIAL OVERVIEW

We will now consider the more important sections of the documents of Vatican II which refer specifically to catechesis. They are paragraphs only and occur in documents which will best be remembered for reasons other than educational issues – there are, in fact, fewer than a dozen explicit references to catechesis in the documents of the council. The first occurs in the Decree on the Bishops' Pastoral Office in the Church:

> Catechetical training is intended to make men's faith become living, conscious and active through the light of instruction. Bishops should see to it that such training be painstakingly given to children, adolescents, young adults and even grown-ups. In this instruction a proper sequence should be observed as well as a method appropriate to the matter that is being treated and to the natural disposition, ability, age and circumstances of the life of the listener. Finally they should see to it that this instruction is based on Sacred Scripture, Tradition, the Liturgy, the teaching authority and life of the Church (Article 14).

This is an important paragraph which deserves close inspection. First of all, it is evident that the view on catechesis is not one of mere instruction in doctrine but is, rather, one which has for its aim at all times, and to diverse groups of people, the broader task of development of faith.

Secondly, there is no supposition that catechesis is something which should only be directed to beginners requiring instruction. Rather, it is pointed out that it is to be given to various age groups at every stage of their lives.

Thirdly, it is indicative of the influence of the human sciences in our day and of the inner consistency of much of Vatican II's thought, that there is emphasis not simply on sequence and method (familiar enough in catechesis) but also on natural dispositions, i.e. the psychological readiness of those to receive or be involved in catechesis. Thus, the explicitly theological follows after the human experience of the recipients.

Lastly, it is here that the actual content of catechesis is specified, viz. Scripture, Tradition, Liturgy and the teaching office of the Church.

In the paragraph cited, the implications of the individual and collective roles of bishops have been considered. This is particularly interesting because the uniform set of directives (the catechism) seems to have been set aside. In relation to 'individual directories concerning the pastoral care of special groups of the faithful, as the different circumstances of the particular nations or regions require', the passage continues:

> A directory should be composed with respect to the catechetical instruction of the Christian people, and should deal with the *fundamental principles of such instruction*, its arrangement, and the composition of books on the subject [*italics mine*].[10]

This, in itself, is a notable development because of the implicit recognition of the possibility that catechesis may have to relate to the nature of the individual. Having due regard for the nature of the individual was a catechetical approach already favoured by St Augustine some seventeen centuries earlier in his discourse *De Catechizandis Rudibus*.

The only other specific references to catechesis in the conciliar documents occur in the Decree on the Missions and in the Decree on Christian Education. The latter document maintains the Church's traditional position of being 'particularly concerned with the means proper to herself, of which catechetical training is foremost' for

> ... such instruction gives clarity and vigour to faith, nourishes a life lived according to the spirit of Christ, leads to a knowing

and active participation in the liturgical mystery and inspires apostolic action (Article 4).

The document also calls for an increase in the number of schools available for catechists to study Christian doctrine and scripture and also to have their work signalised by the bestowal of a canonical mission at a public liturgical ceremony in order to give them greater authority in their work.

In this document on Christian Education, it is useful to note that, although basic principles relating to Christian education are re-affirmed, there is little to suggest any radically new insights. However, the Council did recognise the existence of different local contexts to which catechetical methodologies would have to adapt:

> [educational] principles will have to be developed at greater length by a special post-conciliar Commission and applied by episcopal conferences to varying local situations. [11]

The willingness to accept such diversity is a definite change with regards to catechesis. The principle, it is presumed, should apply with equal validity to differences in age, family background, experiences of faith etc., when a person is being considered in relation to catechesis.

The Decree on Christian Education is also realistic in recognising the diversity of school situations open to pupils, so that it does not proceed simply on the assumption that all Roman Catholic children will necessarily receive their education in Catholic schools, be it the best and ideal situation. In at least tacitly acknowledging the possibility of Catholic pupils in secular state schools, the document recognises the necessity of other agencies to take responsibility for catechesis. It is, nevertheless, difficult to discern a clear statement on a possible means of resolving the necessary tensions between the rights of parents in relation to the religious instruction of their young and the implementation of this right by attention to schools in which there can often be (by necessity) little official concern for catechesis by the Roman Catholic body.

The Decree on Christian Education is an important document because it sets the agenda for progress in catechesis in the post-conciliar era. Mention is made, in the preface, of 'continuing education of adults'. True education is directed towards the 'formation' of the human person (par. 1). The importance of the liturgy as a catechetical tool is recognised (par. 2). The Christian community (par. 5) and Christian society at large (par. 3) have important responsibilities in Christian education. These themes would again be taken up and developed in post-conciliar documents.

Perhaps the most important discussion of Vatican II, and one which is directly related to catechesis, was the discussion on the nature of the Church. The Dogmatic Constitution on the Church, which that discussion resulted in, established new parameters for catechesis. It is towards this document we will now focus our attention.

Vatican II's Dogmatic Constitution on the Church
This document is particularly concerned with the Church's self-understanding and her function. It is in the light of this understanding that the, perhaps, traditionally overemphasised role of doctrinal transmission may best be understood. In this sense no document of the council was of greater importance than the Dogmatic Constitution on the Church, more commonly known as *Lumen Gentium*,[12] in which the Church outlined her understanding of her nature and mission. From every point of view, such understanding is of the greatest importance for those engaged in catechesis to any extent. This is so because it is necessary for catechists' understanding of their mission within the Church as well as for their attitude towards those whom they instruct in the doctrines of the Church, that they appreciate the nature and force of the Church's view of herself.

Thus, it is interesting and indeed necessary to consider the structure and content of this, the longest, document of Vatican II and to point out changes in attitude and self-understanding which are of significance to this work. For purposes of analysis a general sequence of the document is followed below giving special attention to statements or attitudes which are either new or different in emphasis from those previously understood by catechists who were themselves steeped in the vision of the Councils of Trent and Vatican I.

Unlike other councils, Vatican II did not promulgate any new doctrine but it did pay a great deal of attention to reformulation of traditional beliefs in relation to the contemporary world. One final point needs to be made: although this is called a Dogmatic Constitution there is no *a priori* determination of what the Church should be. Instead the language used is essentially biblical rather than legalistic as it had been, for example, in the 1917 Code of Canon Law. This attempt to confine its vision to that of the history of salvation is strongly in accord with the Constitution on Divine Revelation, *Dei Verbum*, and with the general open attitude of looking at the 'real' rather than the 'ideal' situation existing in the world. Such a view is hardly consistent with the doctrinal transmission model of catechesis which had been in place since the Council of Trent in the guise of the Catechism.

The very title of this document on the Church (*Lumen Gentium*), implying as it does the central view of the Church as the presence of God among humanity, is the very antithesis of the triumphalist attitude with which traditional Roman Catholicism claimed a monopoly over the truth. The Church is presented from within the doctrinal setting of the Trinity as the foundation doctrine of Christianity; and it is only from within this doctrine that God's gracious plan of salvation can be known and understood. Here is found the broad sweep of salvation history with its stress on God's preparation for the sending of his Son, not simply to the chosen people of the house of Israel but to humanity in its entirety.

Church as sacrament /sign

The document makes use of the expression (made popular by Karl Rahner and Edward Schillebeeckx) the *Church as Sacrament* — i.e. as a sign and source of grace for humankind. It is by the incorporation of those who receive the gift of redemption through Christ and the Spirit that the union and fellowship of the Church comes into being. In this sense, the union of people in worship, i.e. their acknowledgement of their dependence on the work of the Father, Son and Holy Spirit, is the form of the Church, both in the local sense and in the wider communion that this represents. This understanding is quite important in the different perspectives it casts on the notion of the Church's Mystical Body, the classic affirmation of Pius XII made in his encyclical *Mystici Corporis* in 1943. Unlike the latter, the Constitution on the Church follows more closely the thought of St Paul; the Church is the communion of those redeemed in Christ, and it is the concrete acknowledgement of this in worship which forms the Church in a given situation. From the individual Church, it is possible to envisage the communion of many such bodies, a position expressed in the idea that the Church is a fellowship of people with Christ. Christ is present through the Spirit in the midst of his people. But where *Mystici Corporis* equated the mystical body of Christ with the Roman Catholic Church, this Constitution much more carefully states:

This Church, constituted and organised in the world as a society, subsists [*subsistere*] in the Catholic Church which is governed by the successors of Peter and by the bishops in union with that successor, although many elements of sanctification and of truth can be found outside of her visible structure. (Article 8).

This is a very important change from the traditional attitude, particularly in the light of the narrow interpretation often made by the emphatic utterance in past times of 'Outside the Church there is no salvation'. Later Church teaching is consistent with this broadening frame of reference, particularly in rejecting any tendency to identify the 'kingdom of God on earth' with the Roman Catholic Church. The implications of this carefully stated modification of view-point for catechesis are particularly important, especially with regard to other Christian Churches, as well as to ecumenism with non-Christian religions. This is so because such a viewpoint acknowledges that many elements of the truths of Christianity can be found not only in other Christian denominations but also in non-Christian religions. Thus, catechetical dialogue between Christians and non-Christians is to be encouraged.

Church as pilgrim people of God
Perhaps nothing has seized the imagination of Christians more generally than the description of the faithful as the 'People of God', and as a pilgrim community.[14] Viewed in the broader perspective of the history of salvation, this pilgrim people, like Israel of old, is forever engaged in an ongoing process which seeks truth. In this position she is still able to acknowledge an ideal of holiness to be attained, but is also quite realistically aware of her historical shortcomings as well as her many and continuing failures to live up to this ideal holiness to which all are individually and collectively called. Such a vision of pilgrimage identifies the Church with the various needs of people all over the world in their common quest for justice. Furthermore, a stress which recalls many of the nineteenth century tensions between Church and State reminds members that the Church must always transcend particular cultures and national boundaries in its pilgrimage towards endtime. If Christ is the 'source of unity and peace', this unity is not to be confused with uniformity. Nor is there to be a hierarchy of privilege but only one of service because by baptism the 'common priesthood of the faithful' and the ministerial or hierarchical priesthood are nonetheless interrelated.[15]

Developing this point, paragraph thirteen begins with the statement that 'all men are called to belong to the new People of God'. If the Catholic faithful are regarded as 'fully incorporated into the society of the Church', the Church recognises the many links shared with those Christians not in union with her, and while regretting this absence of complete unity, praises the quality of these Christian Churches, not in a condescending manner, but with a clear recognition of the common heritage shared with them, and of the scandal of disunity. This unprecedented commendation after four hundred years of anathemas and condemnations has been the basis for the Roman Catholic response to the growth of ecumenism in recent years.

As regards the content of catechesis, especially from the negative view of much of the historical apologetics of the past as well as the study of world religions at present, this has major implications to be considered later. Primary among these considerations is the logical view that absolute truth can not be fully attained and therefore can not be expressed in text book fashion.

Further than this, the solicitude of this document extends to those far outside the Christian faith. Anticipating the later public revocations of traditional attitudes towards the Jewish people, the document emphasises 'this people remains most dear to God'.[16] There is mention too of those who acknowledge the Creator, notably the Moslems, 'professing to hold the faith of Abraham'.[17] It goes on to speak of those who, through no fault of their own, do not yet accept the gospel but who strive to follow what they believe is right and who can thereby attain salvation. From this there is a natural progression to a consideration of the missionary work of the Church, of the duty of everyone to respond to the plea to 'preach the gospel to every creature', not, as in the former emphasis, to save the unbelievers from a perdition for which they were otherwise destined, but to try to share the benefits of the gospel with all.

From this document two further insights are selected because of their implications for catechesis: notably those relating to collegiality and to Christian witness.

Principle of collegiality
The discussions on the principle of collegiality readdress the historical lack of balance of Vatican I which, shortened by the outbreak of the Franco-Prussian war, proceeded to define papal infal-

libility without indicating fully its relation to the episcopate generally. The affirmation indicates two aspects of collegiality: the responsibility of the individual bishop to teach, sanctify and govern his Church on the one hand, and on the other the union of individual Churches to form the 'communion of Churches' with the resulting collegial action of bishops on behalf of the Universal Church. This last point, affirmed by the post-conciliar creation of the Synod of Rome for regular meetings with the Pope on behalf of his whole Church, is important for more than its administrative aspect. Perhaps more important in the long run is the establishment of a principle of dialogue between the bishops themselves and the Pope. The former Prefect of the Congregation for Catholic Education, Gregory Baum, has suggested that, perhaps, the true measure and importance of this development will be an important modification of the exercise of authority at all levels.[18]

Christian witness of the people of God
In sections of the Constitution on the Church, there is particular concern with an important source of catechesis, namely Christian witness. The designation of a special section for the laity is meant simply to specify their special duties as the 'people of God'. These who by baptism have been made 'one body with Christ' but who are not in holy orders or members of a religious order 'seek the kingdom of God by engaging in temporal affairs and by ordering them according to the plan of God'.[19] It is interesting to note the positive importance with which the laity are designated in terms of their baptism and their active role within the 'people of God'. This vision is also extended explicitly through the Decree on the Apostolate of the Laity and implicitly in the other documents on Ecumenism, Christian Education, Communications and Missions.

It must be remembered that in the documents on the Church and on the laity the past presumption is absent which implied that any apostolate which the layman shared was by association with that of the official ministers of the Church. Theoretically none of these documents add anything fundamental which was not implied by the description of 'people of God' and 'pilgrim people' but such expressions are, themselves, an indication of a different frame of mind from that implied by the more traditional descriptions in which the 'faithful' were the undifferentiated mass supporting the apex of a hierarchical priesthood.

Secondly, in other sections of the Constitution on the Church and in the Decree on the Apostolate of the Laity, itself, the foundation and justification of the lay apostolate are expressed in biblical terms. As the majority in the Church, the laity share equally in the mystery of the Church and from this viewpoint, other ministries (including those pertaining to ordained clergy) are designated to assist the laity in their common task of spreading the kingdom of God on earth. This is especially a task of Christian witness. The document goes to great pains to stress the inter-dependence of the lay and clerical ministries in terms which are striking:

> Therefore by divine condescension, the laity have Christ for their brother who, though He was the Lord of all, came not to be served but to serve ... They also have for their brothers those in the sacred ministry who by teaching, by sanctifying and by ruling with the authority of Christ so feed the family of God that the new commandment of charity may be fulfilled by all.[20]

This is an important distinction because it is not here a question of the laity simply acting as collaborators with the clergy (be it in the field of catechesis or in any other task) but rather it is an affirmation of the apostolic task of the laity because of the unique responsibilities and influence they have as individuals 'called in a special way to make the Church present and operative in those places and circumstances where only through them can she become the salt of the earth'.

The particular competence possessed by the laity should be availed of for specific tasks within the Church, notably those associated with missionary work and with catechesis. The conciliar perspective makes it possible to see these aspects as major contributions to the parochial life of the Church. The relevance of all of this for catechetics is particularly well-defined in the Decree on the Apostolate of the Laity where the sixth chapter provides a practical programme for catechesis.

Here the lay person is seen ideally as one who is well informed and active in their own society, as one who learns to base his/her life and self-realisation as a Christian upon the continuing guidance of the Spirit and who witnesses to these values by the quality of his/her daily life. Ideally, he/she has a solid doctrinal formation as well as general cultural and practical training, and by pursuing a prudent policy to see, judge and act, he/she helps to further the kingdom of God.

Such training is recommended from early childhood but 'in a special way ... adolescents and young adults should be initiated into the apostolate and imbued with its spirit'. There is a particular duty incumbent on those responsible for Christian education to ensure that this happens, so that within the family, children are made aware of their wider responsibilities within the community and more particularly within the parish. Priests and catechists are considered to have special duties of cultivating this kind of response from the young, especially in those circumstances where young people are unable to receive such formation in Christian schools. Besides the encouragement of Christian knowledge, both for its own sake and as a means of social contact and influence, there is also emphasis on the importance of opposing and counteracting materialism by the witness of an evangelical life.

FROM PEDAGOGY TOWARDS ANDRAGOGY

With the Second Vatican Council the various movements for renewal had come of age. Although the council, itself, had no formal treatment of catechetics, its deliberations mirrored much of what had characterised catechetical thought and also some that challenged it afresh. Specific references in the council documents to catechesis in the narrow sense are, as previously noted, few and far between. However, it is possible to locate and analyse these references and discern an underlining approach to the entire subject. In doing so it is possible to detect the emergence of a change of emphasis away from children towards adults as the primary subjects of catechesis. This coincides with what can be seen as the beginning of a recognition, once again, that Christianity, by and large, is an adult religion and, thus, educational efforts should be directed primarily to the adult community – an understanding, again, rooted in the early Church. The foundation was laid during the council for a fourth major shift in the history of catechetical thought that understood 'adult catechesis as the chief form of catechesis', a claim concretised in post-conciliar Roman documents and one which will be analysed in greater detail in the next two chapters.

In the decree on the Pastoral Office of Bishops there is a reminder that bishops should present Christian doctrine according to the needs of the times;[21] that they should see to it that catechetical training is given to all age groups including adults, since by instruction faith becomes alive, conscious and active[22] and that catechetical directories [not catechisms] should be prepared. In the decree on the Apostolate of the Laity it is affirmed that parents are the first to communicate the faith to their children and all others in their household and that they have the task of training their children to recognise God's love for people.[23] This is likewise stated in the Declaration on Christian Education. Here, the Council restores to parents the task of principal catechists of their children, a task which had tended to become the preserve of clerics during the medieval era.

The right of parents to determine the kind of religious education their children receive in accordance with the parents' own religious beliefs is asserted in the Declaration on Religious Freedom.[24] A passing reference is made in the decree on the Ministry and Life of Priests which speaks of priests as educators (although by no means exclusive ones) in the faith.[25] The decree on Priestly Formation requires that careful instruction in catechetics (among other subjects) be given to seminarians – again adults.[26] Renewal in catechetics is seen as a sign of ecumenical progress according to the decree on Ecumenism,[27] while the declaration on the Relationship of the Church to Non-Christian Religions warns against catechising that would in any way be identified with maltreatment of the Jewish people.[28]

Catechetics is considered part of the adult ministry of the word according to the Constitution on Divine Revelation.[29] There is a passing reference to adult catechumens in the Constitution on the Church[30] but more detailed mention is found in the decree on the Church's Missionary Activity as indeed there is to catechetics in general.[31]

FROM INDIVIDUAL INSTRUCTION TOWARDS COMMUNAL FORMATION

In the light of Vatican II the sacraments are seen as the actions of Christ in his Church – actions which have a catechetical value in the formation of faith.[32] This, by necessity, means the whole community must celebrate the sacraments and that a variety of ministries are needed to facilitate the participation of all the faithful. It is here, above all, that the sacraments succeed (or fail) as instruments in the formation of faith. If the Church – especially in its local expression, the parish – is seen as an institution (which, as already noted, Vatican II certainly does not see it), then the arrangement is quite simple: one goes there to be 'serviced', not to participate, to receive rather than to contribute. Thus, a lone minister in an empty Church will be sufficient to meet these individualistic requirements. Within such an understanding the vast richness of the sacraments are drastically reduced. Ritual becomes dismissed or truncated. Then baptism, for example, as Aidan Kavanagh expresses it, simply legally enrolls one on the 'Divine Welfare'.[33] Confirmation, too, becomes a social entrance into adolescence for the individual. Communion is seen as a private exercise in personal piety. Confession devolves to a do-it-yourself guilt removal. Catechesis does not even get off the ground.

However, if the Church is seen as a community (which Vatican II does see it – as a community of the pilgrim people of God) then celebrations will be public, participatory affairs – not private individuals receiving from a spiritual resevoir. When ritual develops properly people converge to give sacraments expression and meaning. In fact, to be quite theologically accurate it is then, above all, that the community is itself a sacrament, i.e. that the collected assembly is an outward sign of God's wonderful works in Jesus. Then, indeed, the faithful are led to that full, conscious and active participation which is demanded by the very nature of the liturgy and to which the Christian people, a 'chosen race, a royal priesthood, a holy nation, a redeemed people' have a right and obligation because of that priesthood. In the wake of Vatican II all the sacraments have been revised in their ritual expression – revisions which will remain fairly ineffective without a corresponding change of attitude and understanding on the part of both clergy and laity.

Sacraments and faith flourish best in an interacting community. 'Openness to God,' says Eugene Kennedy, 'is mediated always by our human condition ... Faith grows in the context of a relationship to adult believers'.[34] The converse of this is that faith fares ill without a supportive adult community.

This inextricable relationship between adult community, catechesis and sacraments was well understood in the early Church. At that stage catechesis was simply a proclamation of the truth of the resurrected Christ followed by an invitation and exhortation to believe, repent and be baptised:

> Men of Israel, listen to me ... You must reform and be baptised, each one of you in the name of Jesus Christ, that your sins may be forgiven, then you will receive the gifts of the Holy Spirit'.[35]

The first instruction was basic: faith, repentence and baptism. It could afford to be. It was made to a people already steeped in the biblical lore and sensitised by the prophets, especially John the Baptist. But when the message moved to the Gentile world the situation was different. It took many centuries to build up a similar 'atmosphere', a community, a lifestyle, a worldview that could be characterised as Christian.

In the contemporary context, especially in the face of progressive secularisation, the schooling-instructional model of catechising has become predominant. The very concept of 'Christian education' has become joined almost exclusively to the 'school' which provides both the content and the means of instruction in religion. This model, although still enormously active and influential today, has begun to be seriously questioned since it tends to 'teach' 'religion' without reference to the total faith life of the Christian community. This point will be elaborated upon from an Irish perspective, later in Chapter V.

The hidden agenda in all of this endeavour seems to admit children into a Church or maintain them in institutional loyalty rather than lead them to faith. Parents are often told implicitly or, indeed, explicitly to have a hands-off policy in religious matters – the teacher will teach, provide and train in the sacraments. Thus, creeds and dogmas are taught but faith is not necessarily caught. The reason, according to John H. Westerhoff is that:

> We are not called to be incorporated into the Church as one institution among others. God intends that the Church be a unique witnessing community of faith, a converted pilgrim people living under judgement and inspiration of the gospel to the end that God's will is done and God's community comes. The Church is called to be a community of corporate selves interacting with each other and the world as an expression of their commitment to the Lord of history.[36]

In sharp contrast, Vatican II asserted that sacraments and their catechetical structures must be intrinsically related to the Christian community. They are identified as common celebrations of all, by all, and for all. They are seen in the context of a worshipping community that mediates the presence of Christ. They take their meaning, colour, significnce and catechetical force from the context of a people united in faith, liturgically celebrating that faith in sacramental actions. Thus, sacraments can function successfully in the formation of faith when there is a meaningful sacramental liturgy and a parish that is a true community. These aspects are but two sides of the one sacramental coin. They are inseparable and indispensable presuppositions for growth in faith:

> Liturgical actions are meant to be professions of faith; the external enactment of the liturgy is meant to be a true expression of the attitudes of all those in attendance ... Christianity becomes a true community, one capable of sacramentalising ultimate human community in the kingdom of God, in proportion as there is genuine community in faith.[37]

Catechesis must include liturgical celebrations and liturgical celebrations must rely on effective and genuine community. Therefore, the basic issue is not so much the textbook used in the classroom (which, undoubtedly, does have a purpose to serve) but the local parish which makes (or fails to make) the classroom instruction move from head to heart. If the parish, the believing community, is less than it should be, catechesis will always be less than it should be. Books, visual aids and paraliturgies are all important in catechesis, but the real test of effectiveness is mediated by the community when it gathers to celebrate its sacraments.

RETURN TO THE CENTRALITY OF THE LITURGY

In the remainder of of this chapter I will attempt to outline the great importance the council attached to sacred liturgy as a catechetical expression. This will be achieved by examining firstly the importance attributed to liturgy in the life of the Church, as seen in the Constitution on the Liturgy, secondly by noting the catechetical dimension of the liturgy which the council saw to exist and, thirdly, by showing the manner in which liturgy, together with its catechetical dimension, are inextricably related to Christian living.

Vatican II's Constitution On The Liturgy

Despite the greater theological importance of other documents of Vatican II, notably *Dei Verbum*, the Dogmatic Constitution on the Church and the Declaration on Religious Freedom, it was the Constitution on the Liturgy which first brought the influence of the council to be directed towards catechesis. This led to many new innovations.

One such innovation, and perhaps the most remarkable, was the emphasis upon the use of the vernacular. The renewed emphasis upon the 'Theology of the Word' also necessitated widespread changes in the organisation and selection of scriptural readings, so that it was only natural that these be done in the vernacular. Moreover, the central position and organisation of the readings gave new point to the development and emphasis of the homily which, unlike the formal sermon (organised by subjects for the entire liturgical year and based on the catechism of the Council of Trent), was based on increased numbers of scriptural readings and carefully planned around central themes of the history of salvation.

In a remarkably short time, a vernacular liturgy for the Mass and the administration of the sacraments was a reality. This was a logical result of the efforts of the pioneers of liturgical reform from the time of Jungmann in 1936. The return to the use of the vernacular was important in other respects also. For example, it would not have been possible to see much practical implementation for the Decree on Ecumenism without this rapid change over to the vernacular. Indeed, the very search for suitable translations of prayers and rituals provided an ideal starting point for this kind of *de facto* ecumenism which, in fact, had already come of age for scripture scholars who had already begun to work together at international level.

But there were even bigger factors working for ecumenism, for as the celebrant at Mass now needed to be audible, to face his congregation and to be prepared to present a homily on scriptural readings, his particular role of service to the community was better appreciated in terms of function rather than of hierarchy.

The provision for occasional extension of the chalice to the laity and the encouragement of concelebration rather than separate 'private Masses' without a congregation were important advances in themselves but even more so because of the better appreciation of the role of the faithful. It was not long before an expression, which for centuries had hardly been used except with reference to the 'errors of Luther', was again heard by Roman Catholics: the 'priesthood of all believers'.[38] This expression, used in a number of Council documents, related primarily to the liturgy:

> Mother Church earnestly desires that all the faithful be led to that full, conscious and active participation in liturgical celebrations which is demanded by the very nature of the liturgy. Such participation by the Christian people as a 'chosen race, a royal priesthood, a holy nation, a purchased people' (1Pet 2:9; 42:4-5) is their right and duty by reason of their baptism.[39]

THE CATECHETICAL CONCERNS OF VATICAN II

What has been said to this point confirms the opinion of Edward Schillebeeckx who saw the main achievement of this document as follows:

> The fundamental gain of this constitution is that it broke the clergy's monopoly over the liturgy. Whereas it was formerly the priests' affair, with the faithful no more than his clientele, the council regards not only the priest but the entire Christian community, God's people, as the subject of the liturgical celebration in which each in his proper place is given his own particular, hierarchically ordered function – a theological view with all kinds of practical repercussions. [40]

Thus, undoubtedly, a clear return to the liturgical situation of the early Church is discernible – a situation where all the faithful present exercise their Christian ministries appropriate to their charisms.

Another factor with far-reaching implications for catechesis was the practical acceptance of a plurality of forms of religious worship according to the different peoples and regions of the world, a change of great importance for the Church in traditional missionary areas. This kind of adaptation to native cultures which the Jesuits in China and in the East had tried to effect in the sixteenth century was at last accepted and, indeed, recommended. The change, significant in itself and in its recognition of the importance of the native culture, has even greater prominence when considered against the accumulated rubrics of centuries which had regulated even the slightest movements and gestures of the celebrant in the uniformity of the Roman Rite.

The return to a more biblical notion of sacrifice and to the affirmation of the centrality of the Paschal Mystery, together with the 'demythologisation' which accompanied the demise of Latin and the increased understanding made available to all by the use of the vernacular, were collectively responsible for the delegation of certain ministries to the laity. From the view point of catechesis the very involvement of laity in the preparation for, and enactment of, such rituals seemed to lead many to a more profound sense of understanding of the aims and intentions of religious celebration.

In his introduction to the Constitution on the Liturgy, in the the Abbot edition of the documents of Vatican II, McNaspy points out that the spade work for the document had been carefully prepared, so that it was able to channel the kind of thinking which had ebbed and flowed since the beginning of modern liturgical refom with Pius X in the early years of this century.[41] In this sense the document simply made available to the whole Church the kind of thinking which had already developed regionally throughout the Roman Catholic world, especially in missionary lands. An example of this was the recognition of the priesthood of the faithful which was to find expression in the term 'people of God' as used in the Dogmatic Constitution on the Church. One may, therefore, summarise the contribution of this Liturgical Constitution to catechesis by alluding to the renewed attention it gave to the proclamation (*Keryssein*) aspect of the Liturgy of the Word. This revised Liturgy of the Word makes the scriptural education of the faithful at least more likely, especially as the revised series of readings attempt to combine readings from the Old and New Testaments around a central theme of the history of salvation in such a way that over a three year cycle the greater part of the bible is read.

The possibility of catechising within the context of the liturgy was made more likely when the language used was immediately intelligible both by being heard and easily understood. This is not to deny the mystical aspects of the traditional liturgy with its emphasis upon gesture, silence and the centuries of traditional Latin settings in music.

There are indications that the traditional symbols associated with some of the sacraments may be given different forms in mission countries in order to be better appreciated as symbols in the particular culture in which they are used. Perhaps it needs to be stressed that the value of liturgy should not depend on extraneous considerations. As a form of worship, liturgy is an integral dimension of religion, both in the primary sense of offering homage to God and also in the form of communal activity in which such homage is given. As Jacques Bournique says:

> It is the profound intention of the Constitution to make clear the role of the community – a community which is called and gathered together by the Word of God which hears, listens to and assimilates this Word, and is thus able to respond to it ... Liturgy exists at one and the same time for God and for man. It is the homage of God, but it must also involve and transform man, and implies a catechetical dimension.[42]

It is within this catechetical dimension that both pupils and teachers may jointly participate in a common activity involving different forms of learning; the explicitly doctrinal as well as the experiential dimension of social worship.

The catechetical dimension of the liturgy
According to Vatican II the principal goal of liturgical renewal is that '... all the faithful be led to that full conscious and active participation in liturgical celebrations'.[43] This goal of renewal, as stated in the Constitution on the Liturgy, is set forth in the midst of exhortations for instruction on the liturgy to be given to pastors, clergy, professors and students in seminaries and all the faithful. The implication is that the faithful will be led to optimum participation by preparation for celebration through catechesis.

The full, conscious and active participation in the liturgy parallels the living conscious and active faith sought in catechesis. Catechesis and liturgy are so intimately related that one can hardly carry out one of these ministries (which is, effectively, what they are – as will be argued later) without relating it to the other. Catechesis builds faith which leads to liturgy which, in turn, expresses and shapes faith and (hopefully) raises the desire for further catechesis.

In each ministry the community is built up. In each the word is proclaimed, praise is offered to God and all are sent to minister to others. Catechesis is the handmaiden of liturgy inasmuch as the celebration of liturgy is the summit of the Church's activity.[44] The relationship, then, can best be described as a necessary symbiotic one.

The Instruction on the Constitution on the Liturgy issued on September 26th 1964 made such a relationship quite explicit when it said:

> It is especially necessary that there be an intimate union between liturgy, catechesis, religious instruction and preaching.[45]

This is a change from the previous position which made no visible connection between the celebration of the liturgy itself and the catechising of the faithful. Often both were seen (perhaps even unintentionally) to be in opposition to one another. Johannes Hoffinger who was active in both the liturgical and catechetical renewals of pre-Vatican II held this opinion as the following statement shows:

> In shaping the people of God to a true Christianity, an ample and intelligent participation in the liturgy is more efficacious than any kind of catechising ...[46]

The Liturgy Constitution speaks of the liturgy as being:

> The summit towards which the activity of the Church is directed and from which all her power flows.[47]

Thus, catechesis too must be part of the Church's activity directed to this summit and expressible in the liturgy. But this is only part of the understanding of the council in relation to both the liturgy and catechesis. In the above-mentioned Instruction the explicit statement is made that:

> Catechesis is the summit and source of the formation of the faithful.[48]

The formation of the faithful is not to be looked upon in the narrow sense of listening to the homily. However, the Constitution does pay due cognisance to the importance of the homily:

> The ministry of preaching is to be filled most faithfully and carefully. The sermon, moreover, should draw its content from scriptural and liturgical sources, for it is in the proclamation of God's wonderful sources in the history of salvation, which is the mystery of Christ ever made present and active in us, especially in the celebration of the liturgy.[49]

and:

> At those Masses which are celebrated with the assistance of the people on Sundays and feasts of obligation, it should not be omitted except for a serious reason.[50]

However, to view the homily as the sole catechetical dimension of the liturgy would in no way do justice to the insights of this council. Rather, the liturgy by its very nature is the centre, apex and font of every pastoral activity. The end of this pastoral activity (including catechesis) is achieved not exactly by means of the liturgy but more precisely *in* the liturgy. The catechetical dimension of the liturgy is more as a result of doing and participating (as a community) than of listening and 'understnding' as an individual.

The community, in exercising its rights (obtained by way of baptism) as a priesthood of the faithful, at the same time re-enacts and participates in the Paschal Mystery. This mystery is unfolded annually:

> ... principally through baptism and the sacred mystery of the eucharist ... and towards which the other sacraments and sac-

ramentals are ordered as well as the cycle of feasts ... unfolded annually in the Church.[51]

Thus, through the liturgical celebration of all the sacraments it is much more a matter of a Christian community being initiated into the Paschal Mystery than of it learning about it. Therefore, in so far as every sacramental celebration by a community unfolds the Paschal Mystery, every sacramental celebration is necessarily catechetical.

DIRECTIVES FOR THE RESTORATION OF THE ADULT CATECHUMENATE

Even before the council fathers assembled to open Vatican II, Rome had already taken steps to re-examine the catechesis of adults and, where appropriate, under certain circumstances to restore the ancient adult catechumenate. On April 16, 1962, the Congregation for Sacred Rites promulgated a general decree of six paragraphs sanctioning a seven-part procedural initiation of adult Christians.[52]

Basically, what the Congregation did was to divide the existing long service of instruction into its component parts in order to provide progressive stages of catechetical instruction. The broad purpose was a simple one stated in the decree itself: 'To sanctify the catechetical instruction with sacred rites'.

While it was not understood by most commentators at the time as being a radical revision, it was, however, looked upon as more than a stop-gap filler in the serious *lacunae* existing in the Church's sacramental life. It is always difficult to choose the most prominent features in a given example of liturgical reform, but it is possible in this respect to delineate five features of the decree which seem significant.

Again, the generous and more widespread use of the mother tongues in the baptismal liturgy is the first. This decree was not revolutionary on the vernacular front but, when it was promulgated, it was seen as an important break-through. Secondly, the rite itself takes on significance in its spaced timing. The baptismal liturgy was not shortened – that would happen later – but the whole ceremony extending over seven distinct services unfolded gradually with both instruction and developing initiation taking on an experiential meaning which was often lost heretofore. A third feature was the measure of flexibility allowable in the decree. It left particulars of restored arrangements to individual local ordinaries. A fourth improvement was the renewed importance given to the sacrament of confirmation, especially within the context of the total initiation of the Christian. Most revolutionary of all, perhaps, was the involvement of all the members of the local Christian community in the spiritual preparation of the catechumens. Initiation into the Church is understood as a cause for the whole community's concern and rejoicing at parish level. Only if the faithful are able to take a meaningful part in this ceremony can they have a significant recognition of its deep importance to them.

The congregation of Sacred Rites made an important and carefully planned step forward in their decree, but it was left to Vatican II to spell out ideals far beyond their proposals. What could not be done in 1962 became possible in 1965 after the promulgation of the documents on the liturgy and the missions.

The first conciliar impetus in relation to the adult catechumenate is found in the Constitution on the Sacred Liturgy:

> The catechumenate for adults, comprising several distinct steps is to be restored and brought into use at the discretion of the local ordinary. By this means the time of the catechumenate, which is intended as a period of suitable instruction, may be sanctified by sacred rites to be celebrated at successive intervals of time (Article 64).

and

> Both rites for the baptism of adults are to be revised, not only the simpler rite but also, taking into consideration the restored catechumenate, the more solemn rite (Article 66).

The catechumenate envisaged by the fathers of Vatican II was not merely a time for the expounding of doctrines and precepts but, rather, a training period for the whole Christian life. Thus, Christian initiation through the catechumenate ought to be taken care of not only by the catechists or priests but by the entire community of the faithful, especially by the sponsors. Hence, right from the outset the catechumens would feel that they belong to the people of God. Also, since the life of the Church is an apostolic one, the catechumens should learn to participate in apostolic activity, by the witness of their lives and by the profession of their faith in the spread of the gospel and in the upbuilding of the Church.

Not content with prescriptions, the framers of the council documents directed the responsibility of implementation toward themselves. The Decree on the Bishops Pastoral Office in the Church exhorts episcopal leadership in this cause:

> bishops should also strive to re-establish or better adapt the instruction of adult catechumens.[53]

This citation finds its source in an earlier document delineating the bishop's important role in his diocese.

> The bishop is to be considered the highpriest of his flock. In a certain sense it is from him that the faithful who are under his care derive and maintain their life in Christ.[54]

Because it is impossible for the bishop to be everywhere, he appoints pastors who take his place. To them and to the parish community 'in a special way are entrusted catechumens and the newly baptised who must be gradually educated to recognise and lead a Christian life'.[55]

The next chapter, in treating post-conciliar directives on catechesis, will give a detailed analysis of this crucially important rite which emerged in final form in 1972. However, here it is important that the insights and recommendations of the council in relation to the restoration of that adult catechumenate be outlined. The following points are worthy of note in this connection.

1. All of the references to the catechumenate in the council documents are unquestionably clear in that the restoration has to do with adults only. The baptismal rite for infants and post-baptismal catechesis are dealt with in different contexts.

2. In the decree directed toward the missions, Vatican II indicates that the formation of a Christian is very important. The transition through which the aspirant goes must bring with it a '... progressive change of outlook and morals, should manifest itself through its social effects and should be gradually developed during the time of the catechumenate'. Thus, on its own, an intellectual grasp of what Christianity means cannot be sufficient.

3. But neither may the community ignore the doctrinal aspect of formation. The ancient catechumenate was a kind of gradual immersion into the truths and traditions of Christianity. In a way this was also a total immersion for it included experiential knowledge in the setting of liturgical worship and Christian living, doctrinal and moral instruction, historical insights and relationships

in the scriptural mode. The hope for a renewed similar presentation is made in the Council's plea that:

> Catechumens should be properly instructed in the mystery of salvation and in the practice of gospel morality. By sacred rites which are to be held at successive intervals they should be introduced into the life of faith, liturgy and love which God's people live.[56]

4. In numerous citations the council fathers attest to the centrality of the eucharistic liturgy and other sacraments in the formation of the Christian. Those seeking participation in the Church 'should be admitted to the catechumenate by liturgical rites and introduced into the life of the liturgy' declares the document on the missions.[57] Further, each instructional worth is pointed up in the Liturgy Constitution and in the decree on the priesthood. 'No Christian community ... can be built up unless it has its basis and centre in the celebration of the most holy eucharist. Here, therefore, all education in the Spirit must originate'.[58] Immersion in the scriptures is recognisable in many passages, e.g. 'The treasures of the bible are to be opened up more lavishly, so that richer fare may be provided ... at the table of God's Word'.[59] The relationship of baptism to confirmation in the context of the catechumenate is only brought out derivatively in the council documents. The Liturgy Constitution calls for the revision of the rite of confirmation for the purpose of showing its 'intimate connection ... with the whole of Christian initiation'.[60]

5. The ramifications of a broader and renewed role of sponsors (and the entire community at large) in the baptismal initiation is far from complete but beginnings are clear. 'Christian initiation should be taken care of not only by catechists and priests but by the entire community of the faithful, especially by the sponsors. Thus ... the catechumens will feel that they belong to the people of God'.[61]

6. The Church is still concerned with Christians of conviction. In her missions document this is made quite clear: 'In accord with the Church's very ancient custom, a convert's motives should be looked into and, if necessary, purified'. [62]

CHAPTER III

The fruits of Vatican II
POSTCONCILIAR PERSPECTIVES
ON FAITH DEVELOPMENT 1965-1972

INTRODUCTION

It would be incorrect to presume that the Second Vatican Council concluded its work with the issuing of its last decree in 1965. That may have marked the formal end of the assembly of bishops but the work commissioned to the various groups and bodies during the council was now just beginning.

The previous chapter outlined the Church's renewed understanding of itself brought about by the insights of the council fathers. It has been noted that, strictly speaking, catechesis as a topic (adult or otherwise) was not dealt with specifically by the bishops at that point in time. However, the vision outlined by the conciliar decrees was one of the utmost importance with respect to the preparation of further documents relating to all aspects of Church activity – including catechesis.

The aim of the next two chapters, then, will be to analyse the postconciliar Roman documents which relate specifically to faith development – documents which were issued by the authority of Popes Paul VI and John Paul II in the light of Vatican II. I identify three major documents whose catechetical content merits close examination. They include the 1971 *General Catechetical Directory* and the 1972 *Rite of Christian Initiation of Adults* (both the subjects of this chapter). Also attention will be drawn to the 1977 Roman Synod of Bishops which dealt specifically with the topic of catechesis and the 1983 *Code of Canon Law* (both the subject of the next chapter).

THE GENERAL CATECHETICAL DIRECTORY

The *General Catechetical Directory*[1] is, in every respect, a product of the Second Vatican Council. The significance of the fact that it was mandated by the Decree on the Pastoral Office of Bishops and not by the Declaration on Christian Education or by the Decree on the

Apostolate of the Laity cannot be overlooked. Catechesis, a form of the Ministry of the Word, is in its roots and branches a pastoral activity for which the episcopate is primarily responsible.

Background to the Catechetical Directory

The *General Catechetical Directory* represents the work of many contributers working alone and in committees. It is quite impossible to trace the sources for all the material which went into its drafting. However, some are obvious. As expected, the documents of the Vatican Council are the most frequently cited. Next in prominence are the papal encyclicals of Pope Paul VI. The spirit, orientation and much of the content was also shaped by (or if not shaped by, at least had a great affinity with) the catechetical directories already commissioned by the national hierarchies of France and Italy.

Less explicit but not less significant, in shaping the *General Catechetical Directory*, was the influence of the Six International Study Weeks on catechesis.[2] The first International Study Week was organised by Johannes Hoffinger in 1959 and held at Nijmegen. It examined the relationship of the liturgy to catechetical activity. The Study Week at Eichstätt in 1960 (a landmark in the history of modern catechetics) gave the kerygmatic approach a new impetus. It outlined principles for a renewal of catechesis and called for careful planning. Offering a blueprint for the renewal of catechesis as it did, its content is echoed throughout the *General Catechetical Directory*. The Study Week in Bangkok in 1962 introduced the notion of 'pre-evangelisation'. It talked in terms of 'preparing the ground' and 'using a language with which men are familiar'. The study weeks at Katigondo (1964) and Manilla (1967) refined the ideas of the previous conferences, and together with them furnished much of the vocabulary found in Part Two of the *Directory*. Their emphasis on evangelistion, conversion, faith, salvation history, adaptation and the 'anthropological' approach forms the heart of pastoral catechesis.[3] The final International Study Week on Catechesis was held in Medellin in 1968. This Study Week will best be remembered for opening up a new dimension of catechesis – that of political catechesis.

The history of the 1971 *General Catechetical Directory*, from the time it was first suggested by the bishop of Beauvais in the late fifties to its publication in 1971, accounts for and highlights several of the main features stressed in the forward to the *Directory* itself:

1) It grew out of the Decree of Vatican II on the Pastoral Office of

Bishops and is 'chiefly intended for bishops, Conferences of Bishops and all who, under their leadership and direction, have responsibilities in the catechetical field'.

2) As it now stands, the *Directory* is, in large, the product of consultation and collaboration with Episcopal Conferences around the world. It draws from contemporary studies and the thought of recognised experts, albeit mostly European, in the catechetical field.

3) The intent of the directory is 'to provide the basic principles of pastoral theology' – not pedagogical theory. Its stress on pastoral actions puts the *General Catechetical Directory* very much in the mainstream of the modern catechetical movement.

4) It is a directory presenting guidelines for the production of national and regional directories and indirectly for catechisms and other catechetical materials.

The last point needs emphasis lest there be some misapprehension about the purpose and the design of the directory. It is concerned chiefly with the ministry of the Word, focusing more on pastoral action than on principles of eduction. It is an example of a fairly new genre of ecclesiastical writings. The *Directory* represents a studied effort to give an orientation – a direction – to catechetical theory and procedures.

At the conclusion of the International Catechetical Congress in Rome (September 20-25, 1971), after the publication of the *Directory*, Archbishop James Knox of Melbourne, a member of the Congregation for the Clergy, read a statement which was subsequently included in the formal conclusions of that Congress:

> The delegates of the Congress are appreciative of the spirit and intention in which the *General Catechetical Directory* has been published. As Cardinal Wright declared to the press: The basic purpose of the *Directory* is to provide an orientation for religious formation, rather than to establish binding rules. It contains updated orientational guidelines rather than prescriptions. The *Directory* will serve as a basic document meant to be adapted to local cultural and pastoral situations of each country under the guidance of the local Episcopal Conference in consultation with the Holy See.[4]

If on the one hand the *General Catechetical Directory* does not have, and was not intended to have, the imperative tone of legislation; on the other, it is not and was not intended to be a new kind of catechism. G. Caprile makes the point that the architects of the *Directory* faced the issue of content squarely and resolved it by excluding any formulae which in some way might have misled readers to take it for a modified version of a universal catechism.[5]

One of the members of the early catechetical subcommittee preparing for Vatican II has made public some recommendations he proposed in July 1961. The publication of the *General Catechetical Directory*, he was pleased to note, means acceptance of a basic distinction that he advocated: catechetical formulae are one thing; a catechism, that is, content, and a catechism text for students are two others. Something else again is a *Directory* which ought to include all aspects, cultural as well as organisational, of catechesis.[6] While the *General Catechetical Directory* encompasses many sociocultural and administrative aspects of catechesis, the foreword makes it clear that not all parts are 'of the same importance'. It is different in scope and purpose from a 'catechism' however the term is understood.

AN OVERVIEW OF THE DIRECTORY

Recognition of the present catechetical situation
The very beginning of the *General Catechetical Directory* treats the reality of the situation regarding catechesis in general within the Roman Catholic Church. Paragraph six focuses on nominal Christians, persons with no deep convictions about their faith. Because of family or ethnic traditions, they may observe some rituals, but faith does not exercise effective influence on their actual lives. The *General Catechetical Directory* singles out two chief causes of this attitude: religion is regarded as establishment and it depends too much on traditional habits and customs.

The nominal Christian is clearly distinguished from the traditional Christian. The latter also depends on habit and custom, but in that case they are not mere ritual.

The *Directory*'s main concern is not that Christians gain abstract knowledge of the faith or even amass a great deal of information about it. Rather, its principal aim is a kind of experiential knowledge that becomes second nature, imbuing every act, conscious or unconscious, with the dynamism of faith. It also stresses the need for an informed and rationl understanding of faith,[7] but here the emphasis is on sincerity and authenticity, virtues that the simple as well as the sophisticated may or may not have.

Paragraph seven speaks of 'Christian Atheism' in connection with the present situation. 'The word atheism is applied to phenomena which are quite distinct from one another'. There is, for example, the form of 'indifferentism' spoken of in the *Directory*. It represents a type of practical atheism in which any theoretical knowledge of God's existence makes no perceptible impact on one's style of life. It is significant that the *General Catechetical Directory* takes up the question of athesim under the heading, *The Church*. Many Christians are, indeed, practical atheists.

Much of modern atheism, in the words of Karl Rahner, is the 'projection of a question disguised as an answer'.[8] Those engaged in the Ministry of the Word are asked to recognise that often what passes for atheism is a rejection of a caricature of God, the kind of superstitious and semi-pagan expression of Christianity berated by the *General Catechetical Directory* in paragraph seven. A renewal of catechesis demands that the believers transcend inadequate presentations of theism and take measures to counteract the shortcomings in the simplistic interpretations of reality too frequently offered by Christians.

Catechesis: Part of the pastoral mission of the Church
Part Two of the *General Catechetical Directory* sets down the basic premise that catechesis is a particular function of the Ministry of the Word. This point of view, fundamental to the entire work, gives the *Directory* its unity and orientation.

It is essential to an understanding of the *Directory* to note that it consistently uses the word catechesis. Never does 'religious education' appear or any of the other English terms sometimes used as metonyms. Despite popular parlance, few scholars consider religious education and catechesis as synonyms. On the other hand, few agree as to exactly what the differences are. It is suggested with some hesitation, therefore, that religious education is primarily an academic enterprise while catechesis is, as the *Directory* insists throughout, a pastoral activity.

Paragraph 17 is an introduction to the key chapter (Chapter II) of the *General Catechetical Directory*. It explains what catechesis is and does. Catechetical activity is an applied form of the Ministry of the Word, again a pastoral activity. In the abstract, the work of catechesis is distinguishable from evangelisation, liturgical preaching and theologising. In the concrete, however, they are bound together and mutually supportive of one another.

The relationship of catechesis to evangelisation and to liturgy is treated in some detail in the *General Catechetical Directory*. Its relationship to theology, however, must be pieced together from fragmentary references. It suggests that catechesis 'prudently considers the help which theological research ... can give'[9] and that it is 'the task of sacred theology and the various other kinds of exposition of Christian Doctrine' – not catechetics – to indicate the way 'for ordering the truths of faith according to an organic plan in a kind of synthesis ...'[10] At the more advanced levels 'a strong doctrinal heritage' implies 'a degree of scientific theology'.[11] Theology, in this context, is the 'systematic treatment and scientific investigation of the truths of faith'.

Adult catechesis as the chief form of catechesis
Church historians and commentators have noted that there is a marked difference between the catechetical concerns of the early Church and that of the modern. Until the sixth or seventh centuries, catechesis was directed to adults who, having heard the gospel message, knowingly and willingly asked to join the Christian community. The time of preparation for baptism, the catechumenate, lasted several years through a period of 'conversion'. Later, when the practice of infant baptism became universal, the focus of catechesis began to shift to children.

The lament of the *Directory* is not that infants and children are baptised and instructed in the faith, but that catechesis came to focus primarily (if not solely) on children and adolescents. Consequently, the main thrust of catechetical activity became centred on the school with its question-answer method of 'initiation' into the Church. The point of the *Directory* is that the paradigm must rather be adult catechesis.

> ... catechesis for adults, since it deals with persons who are capable of an adherence that is fully responsible must be considered the chief form of catechesis. All other forms, which are indeed always necessary, are in some way oriented to it.[12]

The foreword to the *Directory* says that the goal of catechesis must, of necessity, be the 'presentation of the Christian faith in its entirety'. The 'summary or global formulas' capsulate the entire content of faith. They are developed not by adding successive affirmations (one to another like so many links in a chain) but by nurturing them in the heart of the Christian and by making them explicitly relevant.

The reference to 'divine pedagogy' is an acknowledgement that the goal is something that can be achieved only gradually, with patience and with perseverance. In other words, it implies adult catechesis. One begins with a simple presentation but cannot stop short of a mature faith. Catechesis is, thus, a life's work.

In explaining 'religious pedagogy', D. S. Amalorpavadass says:

> [It] ... cannot be but a process, a gradual one and a continuous one, since faith is not a mere intellectual knowledge of truth but the discovery of a person, and revelation and faith are themselves a life-long process. If every person is a mystery, especially God, and if this mystery is unveiled only gradually man also can have access to it and penetrate it gradually ... No one can say 'I know God' once they have learned by heart the Creed, the doctrinal summary of Christian belief. What we do not know of God is more than what we do know of him. What we do not know of God is more dissimilar than similar to what we know. There is no room for any self-complacency. There is no wonder why mystics and Hindu philosophers so often speak in a negative theology: 'God is not this', 'God is not that'.[13]

Maturity of faith, then, is the goal of catechesis. Thus, catechising minors is not the main task but simply a prelude to the principal movement.

Paragraph 92, in affirming the importance of catechesis for adults, cites their individual and social responsibilities. It identifies a number of particular educational needs of adults in terms of goals and roles:

a) *Leadership Roles.* Christians, declared Vatican II, 'carry on their manifold apostolate both in the Church and in the world'. The Decree on the Apostolate of the Laity continues:

> We wish to list here the more important fields of action: namely, Church communities, the family, youth, the social milieu and national and international affairs.[14]

If the temporal and ecclesiastical orders are to be revivified as humanising environments, it will be done by zealous, idealistic and informed adult Christians participating to the fullest in professional, civic and political life. To do this effectively the kind of knowledge and skills which are part of leadership training become paramount.

b) *Teaching Roles*. As formal religious educational programmes and catechetical activity of all kinds grow more and more dependent on voluntary and part-time help, the involvement of large numbers of paraprofessionals becomes more necessary. Adults who understand the nature and goals of catechesis, something of its problems, means and organisation are more likely to be comfortable and, thus, more effective, in their role as catechists.

c) *Parental Roles*. In recent years the efforts to involve parents in the education and catechesis of their own children have become evident e.g. in the growing number of parent manuals published in conjunction with religion textbooks. The 1971 Catechetical Congress in Rome, in recognising that 'the witness of the adult community is the source and goal of youth catechesis', declared that 'parents should receive assistance in their indispensable role of mediating the faith to their children'.[15] Parent education helps adults become more secure in their tasks by providing the requisite knowledge and tactics for home learning. It is no secret, moreover, that some parent education programs are thinly disguised pretexts for involving adults in self-education – a topic which will be returned to in later chapters.

There are specialists who favour the neologism 'andragogy' to distinguish adult eduction from pedagogy which etymologically refers to the education of children – a concept already encountered. Great advances were made in child psychology and schooling when researchers and teachers ceased looking upon children as miniature adults. There is evidence of comparable advances in adult education where researchers and programmers begin looking on adult learners as mature persons and not grown-up children. Adults have different goals than children. They are motivated in different ways. They have different developmental tasks (e.g. parenthood) and they draw on a greater variety of experiences. Although 'andragogists' espouse diverse learning theories and philosophies of education, they do agree on a kind of functional approach to adult education. There is broad consensus among them on the following points:

a) Adult learning is problem-centred. Adults are motivated to learn by the special challenges described in paragraph 96. Their willingness to submit to the discipline of study is born out of such a felt need, or out of perplexities, doubts and curiosity. Thus, the focus of adult education must centre on the problem as it affects the learner, not as it affects the community.

b) Adult learning must be experience-centred. This is a truism of all education. In adult education it means, moreover, that the learning experience, itself, must be situated in an adult setting; that the experiences fostered by the programme appeal to mature persons; and that the participants be free, even encourged, to relate their life experiences to the problem at hand.

c) The adult learner must clearly define his/her goals, and there must be feedback about progress toward such goals from the learner. Several reasons are offered for this. Individuals have more interest in, and accept a greater responsibility for, enterprises they help create. The success or failure of a programme can be measured only in terms of specific needs and expectations. Adults, unlike children and adolescents, are mature enough to appreciate the fact that planning and learning processes are educational, in themselves, and independent of the content or skills learned.

The catechetical dimension of the liturgy
The *General Catechetical Directory* reinforces what several Vatican documents had to say about the significance of participation in the liturgy as a catechetical methodology. From a pedagogical perspective the *Directory* envisages active pedagogy – learning by doing.[16] Thus, catechesis must promote 'active, conscious and genuine participation' in the sacramental life of the Christian community.

The modern catechetical movement, for a long time, progressed in parallel with the liturgical movement. The two were brought together with their common concern for the ministry of the Word. The first International Study Week held in 1959 at Nijmegen had as its theme 'Liturgy and the Missions'. Even before Vatican II it argued for liturgical renewal. Eichstätt, a year later concluded:

> There is latent in the liturgy a colossal wealth of meaning and a tremendous instructive power ... Therefore, the liturgy should be celebrated in a manner which will bring out to the full its catechetical dimension, and which will enable the people to take an active part in it devoutly and intelligently. Hence, in order that the liturgy may produce its due catechetical effect, it should display its intrinsic excellences by means of its intelligibility, beauty and clarity. Only thus can its full catechetical value be exploited. But this cannot be done unless certain reforms are introduced.[17]

Today, liturgists and catechists themselves repudiate the tendency to 'exploit' the liturgy for catechetical purposes. Worship is an end in itself. There is no denying that liturgical celebrations are part of the larger context of life and that they play a significant pedagogical role in the community, but in the proper order of things catechetical activity must serve the worshipping community and not vice versa. A well planned and patiently executed catechesis is essential if the faithful are to take an active and meaningful part in the prayer life of the community.

Christ, the alpha and omega of catechesis
Paragraph 50 of the *Directory* offers a rather complete Christology. Jesus Christ 'is not only the greatest of the prophets' but is also the mediator and the fullness of revelation. The Incarnate Word of God is 'the supreme reason why God intervenes in the world and manifests himself to humankind'. The supreme event of the whole history of salvation is his 'incarnation – passion – death – resurrection'.

As one pieces together the many references it becomes obvious that the *General Catechetical Directory* endorses a Christocentric catechesis:

> ... the mystery of Christ illumines the whole content of catechesis. The diverse elements – biblical, evangelical, ecclesial, human and even cosmic – which catechetical education must take up and expound are all to be referred to the incarnate Son of God (Par. 41).

The centrality of the Paschal Mystery
In the best tradition of patristic and contemporary thought the *General Catechetical Directory* acknowledges that the 'supreme event' in the history of salvation is the resurrection. Also in the best tradition the *Directory* links the resurrection to Christ's passion and death. They are all facets of the same Paschal Mystery.

One recalls that the documents of the council saw the reenactment of the Paschal Mystery throughout the liturgical year as the summit of all liturgical activity. The *Directory* expands on this theme and makes more explicit the connection between liturgy and catechesis.

Catechetical Responsibilities of the Christian Community
The aim of catechesis, according to D.S. Amalorpavadass, mentioned prior to the publication of the *Catechetical Directory:*

> ... does not consist in imparting religious knowledge or in giving religious instruction ... but in initiating and educating one

into a life of personal community relationship with the Father through the Son in the Spirit and with one another in the world today.[18]

This understanding of catechesis is echoed in the *General Catechetical Directory* where it is presented as the communal task of the entire community. The Directory also prefers to speak of catechising a group in a community rather than catechising individuals. Thus, it appears that the local Christian community is, at the one time, both the subject and object of catechesis. This point will be elaborated upon in greater detail when a catechetical analysis of the 1972 *Rite of Christian Initiation of Adults* is undertaken.

Paragraph 30 of the Directory speaks of the task of catechesis as being that of helping communities mature (spiritually) and of bringing them to conversion. Though the Directory does not use the term, the educational role it attributes to the ecclesial community is, in effect, a description of 'socialisation'. From one point of view, all education is socialisation, that is to say a process by which an individual is initiated into a particular community, educated into its values and ideals and led (at some point) to internalise them and adopt them for their own.

In parts four and five the Directory makes it clear that the learner cannot remain passive during the process of 'formation' – which, interpreted in this way, is another term for socialisation into the Christian community. Thus, the community, itself, must be responsible for the value system (and, ultimately, the faith life) into which it initiates its new (and not always younger) members. Thus:

> Catechesis ... demands the witness of faith, both from the catechists and from the ecclesial community, a witness that is joined to an authentic example of Christian life and to a readiness for sacrifice' (Par. 35).

The Christian community must, according to the Directory, have its foundation built upon the sacraments and especially the eucharist. Indeed, one cannot truly speak of eucharist without community. And, as with all liturgical activities, there is a catechetical dimension associated with the celebration of the eucharist. Here the Directory follows closely Vatican II's statement:

> No Christian community can be built up unless it has a basis and centre in the celebration of the Most Holy Eucharist. Here,

therefore, all education in the spirit of the community must originate.[19]

The Christian community is identified with the community of the People of God.[20] Again the Church, as the People of God, highlights the social nature of salvation. In the *Dogmatic Constitution on the Church*, Vatican II declared 'It has pleased God to make men holy and save them not merely as individuals, without any mutual bonds, but by making them into single people ...'.[21]

Principle of Adaptation
A cardinal principle on which much of the Directory hangs is adaptation. It is stated repeatedly in a variety of ways. 'The ministry of the word is not a mere repetition of ancient doctrine ...'.[22] The message 'without adulteration or mutilation is accommodated to the ability of the people taught'.[23] 'The language will be different for different age levels, social conditions ... human cultures and forms of civil life'.[24] The Church 'must strive to promote a greater accord between the possible formulations of the divine message and the various cultures and diverse languages of peoples'.[25]

From a pedagogical point of view, paragraph 46 may well be the most important in the *General Catechetical Directory*. Admittedly there are established norms 'about the exposition of the content of catechesis ... It is not possible, however, to deduce from these norms an order which must be followed in the exposition of content'. The Directory clearly distinguishes an 'objective hierarchy' of Christian truths and values, but makes no attempt here or elsewhere 'to show a suitable way for ordering the truths of faith according to an organic plan ...'.[26] The most well-thought-out theological synthesis needs adaptation to concrete situations and needs of people. Catechesis has its own dynamic. It must be faithful to the message and helpful to those taught by expressing it in a language adapted to 'the intelligence of the hearers'.[27]

THE RESTORED ADULT CATECHUMENATE

One of the final documents to emerge from Vatican II related to the restoration of the ancient catechumenate. It appeared some five years after the formal close of the gathering of bishops in Rome. This catechumenate for adults was restored and the rites and sacraments of initiation were reformed when, under the Pontificate of Paul VI, the *Rite of Christian Initiation of Adults* (R.C.I.A.)

was promulgated on the Solemnity of the Epiphany 1972 by the Sacred Congregation for Divine Worship.

The *Rite of Christian Initiation of Adults* is the only approved or official ritual for the initiation of adults, having replaced the former *Rite for the Baptism of Adults*. That earlier rite was essentially an arrangement of the *Rite of Baptism for a Child* for use with adult catechumens, most often used in 'mission countries'. The 1972 Rite, however, is an entirely new ritual formed out of the Church's ancient tradition and nearly two thousand years of experience.

It is interesting to note that so significant is the importance of the restored catechumenate, that it was not until several years later that a final approved English translation of the Rite became available. In fact, so important is this document that an increasing number of theologians and educationalists are beginning to regard it as the definitive statement of the council on topics ranging from ecclesiology to missiology. This point will be returned to later.

In restoring the catechumenate, the decree of 1972 emphasised that initiation into a Christian community (and thus implicitly catechesis) is a journey in successive stages, wherein the process of conversion is fostered and its transitions marked by liturgical rites. The stage was set for Vatican II's restoration of the ancient process of Christian initiation. To gain an insight into the significnce of this restored rite of adult initiation it is necessary to trace its development from the moment the council called for its restoration to the moment of actual publication.

Vatican II's mandate for catechumenal restoration
The restoration of the catechumenate was mandated even in the very first document issued by the council on December 4th, 1963, the Constitution on the Sacred Liturgy, *Sacrosanctum Concilium*. It stated clearly:

> The catechumenate for adults, comprising several distinct steps, is to be restored ... the period of the catechumenate, which is intended as a time of suitable instruction, may be sanctified by sacred rites, to be celebrated at successive intervals (Par. 64).

Subsequent paragraphs called for the cultural adaptation of the rites, the revision of the rites of adult initiation, and the reintegration of confirmation into its original context as part of the initiation process.

Later documents added further dimensions. The Decree on the Missions, *Ad Gentes*, traced the spiritual journey of the newcomers describing the periods and thresholds of conversion to Christ. The decree outlines the process: proclamation of the mystery of Christ; conversion and faith, noting that conversion 'should manifest itself through its social effects and be gradually developed during the time of the catechumenate'[28] and finally, sacraments of Christian initiation.[29]

Further, the Constitution on the Church specified that 'catechumens are members of the household of God'.[30] That is, they are already members of the Church, although they are not fully incorporated through the sacraments of initiation.

The primary responsibility for the formation of new members in the local Church rests with the bishop. His is the task of overseeing the re-establishment of the catechumenate as well as the adaptation of the instruction of adult catechumens.[31] Since the purpose of Christian initiation is incorporation into the People of God, the entire community of the faithful, especially sponsors, share in this responsibility.[32]

The task of shaping this conciliar vision into reality was entrusted to the Sacred Congregation for Divine Worship. In a response to that mandate the Congregation issued, in 1972, the decree *Ordinus Baptismi Adultorum*, promulgating the *Rite of Christian Initiation of Adults* (R.C.I.A.).

STRUCTURE OF THE R.C.I.A.

In order that the rite of initiation might be more useful for the work of the Church as well as for individual, parochial and missionary circumstances, it is first presented in Part I of the document in its complete and usual form. This is designed for the preparation of a group of candidates, but by simple adaptation, pastors can devise a form suited to one person.

Part II provides rites for special circumstances: the Christian initiation of children, a simple form of the rite for adults to be carried out in exceptional circumstances, and a short form of the rite for those in danger of death. Part II also includes guidelines for preparing uncatechised adults for confirmation and eucharist, along with four optional rites which may be used with such candidates, and the rite of reception of baptised Christians into full communion with the Roman Catholic Church.

Rites for catechumens and baptised (but previously uncatechised) adults in combination, along with a rite combining the reception of baptised Christians into full communion with the Roman Church with the celebration of Christian Initiation at the Easter Vigil, are contained in Appendix I of the document.

The first of these rites, the Rite of Christian Initiation of Adults is normative. It includes not only the sacraments of initiation (baptism, confirmation and eucharist) but the rites of the catechumenate as well. The remaining rites cover the pastoral needs of particular groups or individual persons.

Adult catechesis as communal journey towards conversion
The *Rite of Christian Initiation of Adults* presents a vision of faith as a developing reality that brings the believer into a relationship with God and with all believers.[33] It contains a vision of the Church as a people brought together by a common experience of conversion and faith in Jesus Christ and gifted with the life of the Spirit through baptism. As a result, they are incorporated into an ecclesial body committed to continuing the mission of Christ in the world through personal and corporate witness of a lived faith.

The process and structures outlined in the RCIA are intended for the formation of new members in all facets of ecclesial life: scripture, doctrine, liturgy, morality and ministry, while gradually incorporating them into full membership. It is not designated simply as a preparation for the sacraments of initition, but rather for a life of faith within the Catholic Church.

To accomplish this end, the Church has re-examined the process through which new members are received. In the immediate past the primary model was convert instruction either individually or in groups. The goal of the teaching method was the transmission of knowledge, that is, of the doctrines held by the Catholic Church. The primary aim was to teach the convert to 'know' the faith.

In the RCIA the model is a *process* of *initiation*. The desired goal, to be achieved over a period of time, is twofold: firstly a personal commitment to Christ and, therefore, to a way of life based on the gospel (which the rite understands by the word conversion) and secondly integration into the ecclesial community. Initiation of this nature takes place in the context of a community. Within that context there are many different roles: sponsors, godparents, catechists, guides, role models, peers and the community itself. All are responsible in varying degrees for the formation of new members.

It is not surprising that the Roman Church, at this transitional point in its existence, would rediscover the importance of Christian initiation. In the universal Church, through the active participation of its members, a renewed identity is being shaped and integrated.

It is in this post-conciliar pastoral context that the Church has opted for the model of initiation as the method of forming new members. Its purpose is the creation of a strong sense of personal Christian identity and community solidarity. On the one hand, through this identity and solidarity the faith of the candidate is shaped and his/her conversion deepened by and within the believing community. On the other hand (and equally of vital importance), through the participation of the faithful in the catechumenal process, the community itself continually renews its own faith and growth by giving birth to new generations of believers.

In the words of the rite:

> The initiation of catechumens is a gradual process that takes place in the midst of the community of the faithful. By joining the catechumens in reflecting on the value of the Paschal Mystery and by renewing their own conversion, the faithful provide an example that will help the catechumens to obey the Holy Spirit more generously (Par. 4).

This paragraph highlights not only the communal nature of initiation, but also the core of Christian faith and the importance of time in the conversion process.

Initiation into the Paschal Mystery
The central mystery of faith is the Paschal Mystery. The death-resurrection of Jesus contains, within itself, the very meaning of Christian discipleship. In its light Christians answer symbolically the great questions of human existence: who God is, the meaning of suffering, of life and of death. It is the Mystery of Faith, that which we believe, celebrate and live in the world and into which we initiate new members. It is the paradigm of Christian spirituality as well as of Christian life styles. Those involved in Christian formation have a particular responsibility to continually deepen their understanding of the Paschal Mystery as revealed in the scriptures, celebrated in the worship of the Church and expressed

in the lived vocation of Christians to be the 'salt, leaven and light of the world'.

The RCIA represents the developmental phases of faith and conversion. The catechumenate is not just a programme but a gradual process in which adults hear 'the Mystery of Christ proclaimed and, thus, consciously and freely seek the living God and enter the way of faith and conversion as the Holy Spirit opens their hearts'.[34] What the rite is calling for is a personal response to the gift of the Spirit. While the communication of the faith of the Church may involve programmed aspects, it is important to remember that a qualitative personal response in the faith can never be programmed. The rite is permeated with language that draws attention to the 'gradual process' of development of faith and therefore, of initiation into the Church. It speaks of periods, or progressive stages or steps; of new beginnings, of a journey of crossroads and transitions, of guides and companions on the way that leads to adult ecclesial conversion. In other words, the rite envisions a journey of faith leading to (but not ending with) full incorporation into the community of the faithful.

OVERVIEW OF THE R.C.I.A.

It is important to note the terminology of the rite. The introduction refers to three steps. These steps are not to be confused with the stages of the initiation process. Rather, as the rite indicates, they are 'steps' or 'doorways', that is, the transition point between each of the stages of initiation. Each step is marked by a liturgical rite, the purpose of which is to celebrate what occurred in the previous stage and to mandate and strengthen the candidates for the stage ahead.

The entire process can be outlined as follows:

Stage 1: Evangelisation and Precatechumenate
   Step 1: Rite of becoming a Catechumen
Stage 2: Catechumenate
   Step 2: Rite of Election or Enrolment of Names
Stage 3: Purification and Enlightenment
   Step 3: Celebration of Sacraments of Initiation
Stage 4: Post-baptismal Catechesis or Mystagogy

To identify the different forms of catechesis involved, a brief analysis of each stage is required. The ideal in each stage, envisaged by the authors of the document, is outlined below.

The Precatechumenate

While the rite of initiation properly so-called begins formally with admission to the catechumenate, preliminary stages to this are regarded as critically important for what is to follow. These preliminary stages are referred to variously as a time for 'making inquiry' and for 'investigation' and 'maturation of purpose' on the part of the candidate.

On the part of the local Church this is a time of establishing trust and communion with the enquirer, of evangelising the seeker by proclaiming '... the living God ... and Jesus Christ, whom he sent for the salvation of all men' (Par. 7).

The precatechumenate is intended to prepare the ground for the prospective convert. It presupposes a faith community of mission-minded members; people who are conscious of their responsibility to evangelise. This is a period of dialogue in which the enquirer comes to a first conversion and initial faith. From the 1972 rite which deals with this stage it is possible to discern several responsibilities of the Church in relation to the enquirers. Firstly, in order to educate, the Church ought to be present. The person who welcomes an enquirer is already a visible presence of the Church. That ought to appear in the quality of personal witness as well as in the concern that the enquirer gradually meets with from other Christians and must too discover a true community. Secondly, the Church ought to be acquainted with the 'hearts' of persons to perceive respectfully the direction of the spiritual dynamism which animates them and the values which motivate their activities. Thirdly, the Church ought to seek to enlighten the enquirer by the proclamation of the gospel message of salvation.

The Catechumenate

The actual period of the catechumenate can last for several years within which the new rite envisions a multi-dimensional catechesis. This involves a) doctrinal formation accommodated to the liturgical year; b) an authentic experience of the Christian community in which the catechumens are formed by living closely with others who are also trying to live the Christian way of life; c) participation in public worship, especially in the liturgy of the Word and d) apostolic involvement, working actively with others to spread the gospel and build up the Church by the testimony of their lives and the profession of their faith. Such catechesis obviously transcends the confines of a classroom or discussion group and holds forth great possibilities of ministry by many members of the parish community.

Perhaps, overall, the catechetical mission of the Church at this stage is best described by the Greek term *matheteusate* which means not merely 'to teach' but 'to make disciples of'. This process takes place in the heart of the community by the instructions, the mutual concern and obligingness (1 Cor 8:1) and by the common liturgy (1 Cor 14).

In fact, the communal dimension is essential to the Church's catechesis throughout the catechumenate. If the catechumenate lasts several years, many vital scriptural and theological attitudes can be absorbed by the catechumen in the midst of the faith community. The local Church offers its faith experience to the candidate through prayer, acts of mercy and concern for justice. However, the actual reality may differ greatly. According to Ralph Keifer:

> The concept of Church as a local communion in faith, as a vehicle of the experience of the presence of the risen Lord and as an eschatological sign, exists only in official texts and clerical rhetoric, not as something perceived by the great majority of Church goers. Our operative model is still that of the established Church, a bastion of conservatism, convention and respectability. We do not conceive of the Church as a dynamic and communal reality but as a static institution ministering to the needs of individuals who present themselves on occasion. The Church is not a 'we' but a 'they' or an 'it'. Minimal conformity, not conversion is the standard by which Church life is measured. That this conversion should be a matter of actual experience, and even of corporal experience, is not expected and not really wanted.[35]

If this analysis of Keifer is valid for many parishes, then a great deal of attention will have to be given to improving the ecclesial conditions into which one invites the catechumen. Preparing to celebrate the new rite properly may well serve as an incentive to renew local faith communities. The catechumenate can become a privileged time for the mutual promotion of the Christian community and of the catechumens.

In effect, then, the catechumenate is not a school but an initiation. The difference is that a school has some students who learn a lesson, initiation has some disciples who discover a way of life.

Catechesis is neither a lesson nor doctrinal, moral or sacramental information. Rather, it is an experience in the course of which the candidate is initiated into the social and cultural life of a local ecclesial community. Catechesis consists of facilitating a change that, in Pauline language, represents the passage from the 'old man' to that of the 'new'.

The liturgical catechesis during the time of preparation for reception of the sacraments of initiation is profoundly biblical: the initiative of God who speaks to humankind and the response of those who move through the process of conversion. The catechist helps to bring out the essential message of the gospel in such a way that genuine conversion can take place. The candidate for baptism must be confronted with what scripture calls 'the way'.

In relation to the catechetical role of sponsorship, Michael Dujarier distinguishes between those of communal and personal sponsorship for the catechumen. The whole Christian community exercises a 'collective sponsorship', a feeling of sponsorship which all the faithful who make up the parish community ought to sense. The personal sponsor must be, at the same time, a witness and a guide:

> As a witness to Christ, he witnesses in his daily life for those men of goodwill, who are seeking God, and he will continue to do this throughout their catechumenate, since converts need to see the gospel actually being lived by men like themselves to be sure that the Church really is the bearer of the riches she claims to possess and hand on. As guide, the sponsor is responsible for introducing his/her godchild into the City of God (image made famous by St Augustine), for showing him/her the usages and customs of the people of which he/she is becoming a member.[36]

The ecclesial significance of the sponsor should also be emphasised – the laity participating actively in the mission of the Church, bringing the catechumens into contact with their families, their friends and their faith community.

Ordinarily the catechumenate is to last 'several years', and its content is described in paragraph 19 as consisting of pastoral formation accomplished through 'suitable discipline'. What is to be discerned in the catechumen during this period is not so much intellectual adequacy regarding concepts having to do with faith but rather a maturation in one's disposition towards the faith as a reality lived in common. The whole local Church is to engage rigorously in the maturation process in four ways:

a) First, there is doctrinal formation by presbyters, deacons, catechists and other professional competent lay persons to enable the catechumens to attain a '... suitable knowledge of dogmas and precepts' and '... intimate understanding of the mystery of salvation'.[37] This formation is to be accommodated to the liturgical year and enriched by seasonal celebrations of the Word. Thus, what is envisaged is not merely a classroom effort in watered down theology but a well rounded formation programme that is suffused with a strong liturgical methodology. The document is clear on the purpose of catechesis: it is to form Christians who have something to repent of and celebrate, and who know how to do both in common.

b) Secondly, catechumens are to be formed by living closely with others who know well the demands and advantages of a Christian way of life. The exemplary role of sponsors, godparents, and the whole local community of faith is paramount in this mode of formation. One learns how to fast, pray repent, celebrate and serve the good of one's neighbour less by being lectured to on these matters than by a close association with people who do these things with regular ease and flair.

c) Thirdly, and rather as a specification of the second way, the catechumens' regular participation in public worship eases them gently over a considerable period of time into a sacramental way of life:

> Ordinarily, however, they are present in the assembly of the faithful, they should be dismissed in a friendly manner before the Eucharistic celebration begins ...; they must await their baptism, which will bring them into the priestly people and to ... the Christian worship of the New Covenant (Par. 19:3).

This means that while catechumens are regarded as Christians, their not yet being 'of the faithful' should be manifested visibly in the worshipping assembly. The dismissal of catechumens before the Prayer of the Faithful and preparation of the gifts may, in addition, serve as an effective nonverbal catechesis for the faithful on the awesome dignity of their own baptism. To emphasise the real importance of this act, it will be necessary to evolve some ritual form of dismissal – perhaps the community prayer of the catechumens, once again found in the Roman Rite.

d) Fourthly and finally, 'Since the Church's life is apostolic, catechumens should also learn how to work actively with others to spread the gospel and build up the Church by the the testimony of their lives and the profession of their faith'.[38] From this it is again obvious that catechesis, in the spirit of the document, goes far beyond the classroom and its instructional techniques. What is envisaged here is not only formal 'religious education' but an ecclesiology of social action in evangelisation.

Period of Purification and Enlightenment
When it appears to the satisfaction of all those immediately concerned (local clergy, catechists, sponsors and godparents acting on behalf of the community) that a catechumen has attained by grace and effort a conversion of mind and life, a sufficient knowledge of Christian teaching and a sense of faith and charity, he or she may be elected by the local Church to enter proximate preparation for the sacraments of initiation when next these are to be celebrated.[39] The period of preparation is called a time of Purification and Enlightenment.[40] It is to be understood more as a period of spiritual recollection than of additional catechesis and is intended to 'purify minds and hearts by the examination of conscience and by repentance and also to enlighten by a deeper knowledge of Christ the Saviour'.[41] This time coincides usually, if not always, with Lent – a season which, in its ethos, liturgy and choice of readings, prepares for reconciliation of existing penitents on Holy Thursday and Good Friday and for sacramental initiation of new members during the Easter Vigil.

The liturgical structure given to the period of purification and enlightenment is very explicit in the document. The act of electing catechumens for sacramental initiation is said to belong to the whole local Church, and it is to be done publicly, after the homily at the main eucharistic celebration on the first Sunday in Lent.[42] Those chosen, the elect, are then publicly scrutinised on their intentions and exorcised[43] after the homily at the main eucharistic celebrations on the third, fourth and fifth Sundays in Lent. They are also formally presented with the Creed and the Lord's Prayer at public celebrations during weekdays late in Lent, being expected to 'give each back' by publicly reciting them at a later service.[44]

Post-baptismal or Mystagogical Catechesis
The chosen catechumens, having passed successfully through the stage of purification and enlightenment, celebrate the sacraments of Christian initiation during the Easter Vigil, the most solemn

feast of the Church's year. The community of faith which, during Lent, had been praying and doing penance for and with the candidates, now renews its own baptismal commitment in a spirit of joy along with the newly baptised. Following this Easter celebration, the Church continues to offer post-baptismal catechesis to strengthen the first steps of the new Christians (now known as *neophytes*). The rite describes what is intended:

> The community and the neophytes move forward together, meditating on the gospel, sharing in the eucharist and performing works of charity. In this way they understand the Paschal Mystery more fully and bring it into their lives more and more ... (Par. 37).

This new frequenting of the sacraments enlightens the neophytes' understanding of the Holy Scriptures and also increases their knowledge of men and develops the experience in the community itself. As a result, the relationship of the neophyte with the rest of the faithful becomes easier and more beneficial. The time of post-baptismal catechesis is of great importance so that the neophytes, helped by their sponsors, may enter into a closer relationship with the faithful and bring them renewed vision and a new impetus (Par. 39).

IMPLICIT COMMUNAL MINISTRIES OF THE RITE

The restoration of the catechumenate calls for the collaboration of many ministries (both ordained and non-ordained) in the local ecclesial community. It has been shown that the whole community is called upon to participate, but some members, in particular, will serve as sponsors and as catechists. One can involve the enthusiasm of young adults as well as the wisdom of senior citizens, the prayers of the shut-ins and the witness of the suffering and dying parishioners. Bishops, priests and deacons also have important ministries to serve throughout the multi-dimensional catechesis. Finally, one must remember that the catechumens likewise minister to the existing faithful:

> As a group, catechumens occupy an important place in Church life not only because they are recipients of the Church's faith in a passive way through the catechetical teaching process. They also function as a corporate presence, witnessing constantly to the Church and her continuing need for conversion to Christ. Without this sustained corporate witness the Church is found

to be more sluggish in her own conversion and more resistant to change in general.[45]

IMPLICATIONS OF THE RITE

The 1972 *Rite of Christian Initiation of Adults* has various theological, pastoral and catechetical implications, some of which are included below:

1. Catechesis as initiation is a process and is to be considered a priority of the local faith community.

2. The Christian initiation of adults, fully celebrated, is theologically and catechetically normative.

3. The whole faith community is to be involved in this dynamic process of initiating new members.

4. Initiation is twinned to the liturgical-sacramental life of the Church.

5. In striving towards conversion in a local Christian community, the faith life of that same community is deepened and renewed in the one process.

6. Catechesis is to be understood as being multi-dimensional. It includes certain thresholds and significant moments with liturgical rites which correspond to them.

7. Apostolic activities, ascetical practices, prayer and works of mercy are all parts of the Church's evangelical mission and catechumenal process.

8. Catechists and sponsors must be concerned not merely with doctrinal and ecclesiastical data but also with the profound call to conversion.

9. Catechumens are joined to the Church as an Order, exercising their special charisms.

10. The sacraments of baptism, confirmation and eucharist are seen in their interrelatedness as sacraments of initiation within a total process of initiation.

CHAPTER IV

The fruits of Vatican II
POST-CONCILIAR PERSPECTIVES
ON FAITH DEVELOPMENT 1973-1993

INTRODUCTION

The twenty year span 1973-1993 will, in the area of catechesis, best be remembered for two notable events. Firstly, there was the important 1977 Synod of Bishops in Rome which was devoted mainly to the topic of catechesis. This synod adapted and synthesised many contemporary thoughts and formulations which related to catechesis. Secondly, the Code of Canon Law (the Church's legal constitution) was revised. The new code, emerging as it did in 1983, replaced one which had been operative since 1917. It issued revised regulations concerning catechesis which, in general, reflected closely the insights of Vatican II.

The aim of this chapter, then, will be to examine these two further dimensions of post-Conciliar catechetical recommendations and legislature. Finally, the possibility that a U-turn away from Vatican II's recommended catechetical methodology is currently underway in the contemporary Church will be investigated. This will be done by reference to the Universal Catechism project.

1977 SYNOD OF BISHOPS ON CATECHESIS

The fifth Synod of Bishops, which gathered in Rome from September 30th to October 28th 1977, discussed the Church's catechetical mission. The greatest value of this Synod, according to Dublin's Bishop Donal Murray, lay '... not in its documents, but in the event itself'.[1] By this he meant that the significance of the Synod was less due to the value of the documents produced or conclusions drawn than to the fact that Pope Paul VI thought it sufficiently important to hold a General Synod on the subject in the first place.

In fact, the documents produced by the Synod reveal little new in the line of catechetical methodology which catechists had not already been aware of previously. According to Murray, the synod:

> ... was not designed to come up with answers that nobody ever

thought of before. If, on reading through the documents, one feels that they say little that catechists have not already been saying for years, it is surely a matter of satisfaction that these are the things that the bishops have listened to and called to the attention of the Church at large. [2]

Perhaps equally relevant to the present study are some of the preparatory documents and the submissions of many of the world's bishops. For example, Cardinal Leon-Joseph Suenens, on behalf of the Belgian Episcopal Conference, emphasised the 'necessity of seeing catechesis vehicled and sustained by living Christian communities' and that 'a Christian is not completely evangelised unless he himself becomes an evangeliser'. In a more interesting proposal he suggested that the synod should:

> ... examine a suggestion made at the 1974 synod, regarding the necessity of founding a neo-catechumenate for adults who, having been already sacramentally baptised and confirmed, must be helped to undertake their previous commitments with full personal responsibility.[3]

Other suggestions, like those from the superior of the Jesuits in Rome, Pedro Arrupe, drew attention to the inter-related areas of catechesis and inculturation, suggesting that efforts must be made to accommodate catechetical methodologies to different cultures throughout the world.

Having carefully noted all the submissions the synod, from the very beginning, found its main concern to be that of formulating an exact strategy to cope with the growing problems in the field of contemporary catechesis. The opening address by Paul VI in the Sistine Chapel on the first day of the synod outlined his deep concern with the existing catechetical situation in the world when he spoke of today's humanity, towards which the Church's pastoral activity is directed:

> ... a humankind that to all appearances is hostile, indifferent and deaf to our words, even though, in fact, one can often detect in this attitude an unconscious yearning, a real and deeply felt search for God.

> [Humanity is] convinced wrongly that the immense progress of rational civilisation, the result of technology and science, removes the need for religion.[4]

A deeper understanding of the entire field of catechesis can be gleaned from the synod's working definition of the word itself. According to the synod, catechesis is:

> ... the activity by which God's word is constantly spread in a living and effective way, leading to a deeper knowledge of the person and the saving message of our Lord Jesus Christ. Through an ordered and progressive education in the faith it leads to a continual process of maturing in the same faith.[5]

Concern for adult faith development
From this understanding one can immediately grasp the reality that minors are by no means to be considered the only recipients of catechesis. Quite specifically the Synod stated that:

> Catechesis must address itself to the children, young people and adults of this present world as it is.[6]

The synod drew its attention to the fact that there are three major (and inter-related) aspects of catechesis i.e. it is *word*, it is *memory* and it is *witness*.

In connection with catechesis as proclamation of the word, the synod made the powerful conclusion that:

> The model for all catechesis is the baptismal catechumenate, that special formation which prepares an adult convert for the profession of his baptismal faith during the Paschal Vigil.[7]

Liturgical and communal dimensions of catechesis
In relation to catechesis as memory, the synod, yet again, reaffirmed that an intimate connection exists between catechesis and liturgy: 'catechesis is connected to the entire sacramental and liturgical life [of the Church]'.[8]

When treating the model of catechesis as witness, the communal dimension of catechesis was outlined:

> Catechesis, in so far as it is witness, educates Christians to take their full place in the community of disciples ... which is the Church.[9]

However, the role of the community in relation to catechesis is greater than just that of witness. Again, 'Catechesis is not simply an individual task, it is carried out in the entire Christian community'. The bishop has the primary role but along with him '... all in their own way must collaborate in the ministry of catechesis'.

The content of catechesis
Regarding the content of catechesis the synod followed the line of

thought of Vatican II which recommended the usage of the *Catechetical Directory* (published in 1971) as opposed to a possible future Universal Catechism of Doctrine. However, an analysis of the documentation of this synod indicates that there was some contention between bishops whose orientation was 'academic' and those who were more 'pastorally' inclined.

Those preoccupied with an academic viewpoint were very interested in content, traditional formulations of doctrines and the teaching authority of the magisterium. They wanted to be sure that the entire Christian message was being preached, and in a way that they and their people could recognise. Of the two hundred delegates a 'few isolated voices' proposed a new Universal Catechism.[10] Such a catechism, they hoped, would be something like the Catechism of the Council of Trent and would, hopefully, provide some kind of control over elements in current catechesis which had produced confusion and discontent among some members of the Church.[11]

The bishops who were more pastorally inclined shared the concern of the others about integrity of content and the need to calm confusion. But their analysis of the causes and proposals for cure were quite different. As American bishop Raymond Lucker pointed out, the solution to contemporary problems is:

> ... not a new catechism or even a source book. We already have a General Catechetical Directory, National Catechetical Directories, the Credo of the People of God, the Documents of Vatican II and the pastoral letters of bishops. They are all excellent, but they have not solved the problem.[12]

The idea of a Universal Catechism which would be normative for the whole Church was, in the end, firmly ruled out by the synod.

Conclusions of the 1977 synod
The 1977 Synod of Bishops reaffirmed several conciliar precedents already established in relation to catechesis: firstly, the chief form of catechesis ought to be that of adults; secondly, all members of the community have catechetical responsibilities; thirdly, catechesis must be linked to the communal celebration of the liturgy and, finally, the difficulties encountered in relation to the content of catechesis would not be solved by the compilation of a Master or Universal Catechism.

THE 1983 CODE OF CANON LAW

Much of the material relating to the Church's teaching capacity in the present Code of Canon Law (promulgated under the authority of Pope John Paul II, January 25th, 1983) has no parallel in the 1917 Code which it replaced. The new legislation is derived from the documents of the Second Vatican Council, especially the decrees and declarations that relate to the Church's pastoral ministry: The Church's missionry activity, *Ad Gentes*; The bishops' pastoral office in the Church, *Christus Dominus*; Christian education, *Gravissimum Educationis* and the instruments of social communication, *Inter Mirifica*. At the more theoretical level, it draws its theological foundations from the dogmatic constitutions on revelation, *Dei Verbum* and the liturgy, *Sacrosanctum Concilium*. This section of the Code draws on three other documents, each in its own way dependent upon Vatican II, which situate the canons in the mainstream of the modern catechetical movement, namely the *General Catechetical Directory*, the apostolic exhortation of Pope Paul VI on evangelisation, *Evangelii Nuntiandi* and that of Pope John Paul II on catechesis, *Catechesi Tradendae*.

Many of the eighty-six canons that make up the section dealing with the Church's teaching capacity (Book III) are exhortatory and declaratory rather then explicitly regulatory or prohibitionary. They are to be taken seriously precisely because they describe the fundamental work of the Church. They deal both with the goals and objectives of the Church's teaching office and with some of the means for reaching them.

Book III of the Code signals its ministerial priorities in the very order it gives the five headings that are seen as constitutive of the Church's teaching office. First and foremost there is the Ministry of the Word which includes both preaching and catechesis. Closely linked with this is the second, The Missionary Activity of the Church. The Church, by its very nature, is missionary and the work of evangelisation is a basic responsibility of all the people of God who share in the missionary call of the Church. These two areas are integral to the nature and mission of the Church and foundational to the other three headings treated in Book III of the Code, i.e. *Catholic education, instruments of social communication* and *profession of faith*.

Ministry of the word
The heading of the first chapter in Book III is 'Ministry of the Di-

vine Word'. It is the thread which runs through all the canons of this section and gives it an intrinsic unity. By way of introduction, canons 756-759 make it clear that proclaiming the gospel is the common task of all Christians, though it assigns responsibilities according to one's office and status in the Church.

Canon 756 states that the Roman Pontiff and the college of bishops have the responsibility for the universal Church. Individual bishops exercise responsibility in particular dioceses under their care. They are designated 'moderators of the entire ministry of the word'. While this implies a general oversight and a singular responsibility, the other canons make it clear that it is a shared task that involves all the the faithful by reason of baptism and confirmation.[13]

The new Code presents a radical restructuring and simplifying of legislation governing the Church's preaching ministry. It is very different from the 1917 law in letter and spirit. 'Sacred ministers are to value greatly the task of preaching since among their principal duties is the proclaiming of the gospel of God to all'.[14] Since it is the word that brings the people of God together – which *makes* the Church – nothing has greater priority.

In keeping with Vatican II's recognition of the central importance of all members of the Church in presenting and handing on the gospel, canon 766 envisages laypersons preaching in churches and oratories. Such preaching is permitted when circumstances require it, for example, when a parish or mission is entrusted to a lay catechist or associate pastor or when, in some cases, it is simply 'useful'.

> Lay persons can be admitted to preach in a church or oratory if it is necessary in certain circumstances or if it is useful in particular cases according to the prescriptions of the conference of bishops (Canon 116).

No special ministerial faculties are required, but the wording of the text indicates that permission is required. This permission could be presumed or implicit in an appointment to a pastoral office; in other circumstances it might be explicit. Permission comes from the bishop, as well as from pastors and rectors of oratories who have the responsibility of providing for the proclamation of the word of God to the people of God. The canon presumes that episcopal conferences will set norms for preaching by the laity.

Canon 766 represents a U-turn from the stern prohibition of the 1917 Code.[15] The ban on lay preaching had a long history going back to the time of Pope Leo the Great in the year 453 and was reiterated in various forms by popes of the thirteenth and fifteenth centuries. The prohibition was aimed at self-appointed preachers, not always orthodox, who were critical of the Church's position regarding points of doctrine and social issues. The dangers presented by the self-appointed, charismatic preacher remain but they are outweighed by today's need for Christians in every walk of life to proclaim the gospel not only by witness but also in word. This dramatic change in the legislation is facilitated by the fact that in many places there are laity committed to the Church, familiar with the Bible, trained in theology and skilled in communication.

However, one restriction on lay preaching is legislated by the code itself. Canon 767, an entirely new text based on the documents of Vatican II, sets down norms for the homily: 'It is part of the liturgy itself, and is reserved to a priest or deacon'. The implication is clear; lay persons are not to preach in that particular form. The homily referred to in this canon is that preached within the eucharistic celebration, as is clear from the context (paragraphs 2 and 3 refer explicitly to the Mass).

This distinction is worth noting because lay persons are permitted to read a homily at sacred celebrations of the word of God when there is no priest or deacon available. Nor does it exclude other forms of preaching by the laity when necessity requires it or usefulness urges it, even in the context of the eucharistic celebration. The *General Instruction of the Roman Missal*[16] states: 'The homily should *ordinarily* be given by the celebrant himself' (*italics mine*).

Catechetical formation
The catechetical task of the Church is explicitly addressed in seven canons, numbers 773 to 780. The first (canon 773) assigns responsibilities and describes relationships among various members of the Church community that should build up and effectively pursue its mission. The 'pastors of souls' (e.g. bishops, pastors of parishes, chaplains etc.) have a serious responsibility for the catechetical formation of the faithful. The catechetical task is part and parcel of their pastoral charge.

> There is a proper and serious duty, especially on the part of pastors of souls, to provide for the catechesis of the Christian

people so that the faith of the faithful becomes living, explicit and productive through formation in doctrine and the experience of Christian living (Canon 773).

The first part of canon 773, the basic assignment of responsibility, is virtually the same as canon 1329 of the 1917 Code. The second part of the canon, however, is new. It helps one understand what catechesis is and how it is accomplished. Catechesis is that form of the ministry of the word directed towards those who have been evangelised, who have heard the gospel and have responded to it in faith. Based on a passage in *Christus Dominus*, the aim of catechetical formation is to render the faith lively, conscious and effective[17] which is to say, catechesis helps faith develop and grow so that it can be a real guiding force in the believer's life. This inclusive understanding of catechesis reflects the position of Pope John Paul II in *Catechesi Tradendae* when he stated that:

> ... the name catechesis was given to the whole of the efforts within the Church to make disciples, to help people to believe that Jesus is the Son of God, so that believing they may have life in his name (Jn 20:31) and to educate and instruct them in this life and thus build up the Body of Christ (Par. 1).

Canon 773 calls for this to be accomplished by means of doctrinal instruction and (here the canon goes beyond *Christus Dominus* and the *General Catechetical Directory* in a significant way) by the experience of Christian living. Faith is nurtured in the actual living of it in the Christian community. One observes the lifestyles and activities of other Christians and interacts with them – in families, neighbourhoods, parishes, schools etc. – as well as by more formal education in the teachings of the gospel.

Sharing the responsibilities
The remaining canons in this section (i.e. canons 774 - 780) make explicit what is implicit in canon 773, namely, that the responsibility for catechetical formation of adults and children is shared by many others in addition to 'pastors of souls'.

In fact, every member of the Christian community shares in the responsibility for the catechetical effort. So vital is this activity to the health and vigour of the Church that it must be the concern of every believer. This new canon is based on the participation of all believers in the prophetic office of Christ.[18] *Catechesi Tradendae* was explicit in assigning the different roles according to one's mission (Pars. 62-69).

Under the supervision of legitimate ecclesiastical authority this concern for catechesis pertains to all the members of the Church in proportion to each one's role (Canon 774 n.1).

Parents have a primary responsibility for the growth in faith and Christian living of those to whom they have given the gift of life. The substance of this paragraph was contained in canon 1335 of the 1917 Code, but the primacy of the parental role has now been made explicit. It is further emphasised by the location of the canon ahead of those which specify the responsibilities of the bishop, pastor, religious, etc. The revised canon finds its roots in conciliar and post-conciliar teachings. Perhaps most influential is *Catechesi Tradendae* which provides an expanded description of this familial catechesis.

> Parents above others are obliged to form their children in the faith and practice of the Christian life by word and example; godparents and those who take the place of parents are bound by an equivalent obligation (Canon 774 n.2).

Those who function *in loco parentis*, either temporarily or permanently, share the same responsibility. This might include adoptive parents, foster parents, custodians, directors of boarding schools and others entrusted with the care of children. It also applies to those who volunteered at the children's baptisms to serve as their godparents.

Canon 775 n. 1 spells out the responsibilities of the diocesan bishop and of the Bishops' Conference in reference to the catechetical task. It has no parallel in the 1917 Code and is, again, based on conciliar and post-conciliar instructions (*Christus Dominus*; the 1979 encyclical *Catechesi Tradendae* and the 1971 *General Catechetical Directory*).

The first paragraph itemises three responsibilities of the individual diocesan bishop: to issue norms for the catechetical effort within the diocese, to see to it that appropriate catechetical materials are made available for the task and to promote and co-ordinate the various catechetical undertakings in the diocese:

> While observing the prescriptions of the Holy See, it is the responsibility of the diocesan bishop to issue norms concerning catechetics and to make provision that suitable instruments for catechesis are available, even by preparing a catechism, if such seems appropriate, and by fostering and co-ordinating catechetical efforts (Canon 775 n.1).

Usually the bishop will carry out these responsibilities through an office of religious education or the diocesan catechetical office, the establishment of which was called for as early as 1935 in the decree *Provido Sane* and, later in 1971, by the *General Catechetical Directory*.

Canon 775 n. 2 assigns to the national conference of bishops the responsibility of seeing that catechisms are published for use in its territory. It is clearly facultative, not mandatory ('if it seems useful'), and implies that the conference could publish catechisms itself or could encourage others to do so. It seems an anomaly that the canon should direct an episcopal conference to obtain the prior approval of the Apostolic See if it publishes a catechism or causes one to be published, whereas if others publish them only the approval of the local ordinary is required. [19]

Apparently the reason for this greater caution and higher review is the official, or semi-official, status that might be attached to a publication which emanates from an episcopal conference. This directive seems to be based on the encyclical *Catechesi Tradendae*[20] which also reminds one that the standard reference for all catechisms is the *General Catechetical Directory*.

> It is the responsibility of the conference of bishops, with the prior approval of the Apostolic See, to see to it that catechisms are issued for its territory if such seems useful (Canon 775 n.2).

Canon 775 n. 3 simply suggests that the episcopal conference may set up a catechetical office as an aid to the catechetical ministry of the individual dioceses. This too was recommended in the *General Catechetical Directory*.

> There can be established, within the conference of bishops, a catechetical office whose principal task would be to furnish assistance to the individual dioceses in catechetical matters.

Canon 776 specifies the responsibilities of the pastor in reference to the religious education of his people. Every baptised person shares this responsibility, but the law says that 'in virtue of his office the pastor is bound to provide for the catechetical formation of adults, young people and children'. He is also to promote and foster the role of parents in family catechesis:

> In virtue of his office the pastor is bound to provide for the catechetical formation of adults, young people and children, to which end he is to employ the services of the clerics attached to the parish as well as of members of institutes of consecrated life

... with due regard for the character of each institution, and lay members of the Christian faithful, above all catechists. All of these are not to refuse to furnish their services willingly unless they are legitimately impeded. The pastor is to promote and foster the role of parents in family catechesis mentioned in Canon 774 n. 2 (Canon 776).

The canon begins by establishing the pastor's obligation, which stems from the office he holds. Many others share this responsibility for the religious formation of the people – in fact every baptised person does – but the law fixes the central and co-ordinating responsibility at the parish level on the pastor.

The 1917 Code mentioned only children as the objects of the pastor's catechetical concern. The new text clearly says that this concern must extend also to both adults and young people. This itemisation clearly implies the need for different kinds of instructional programmes for each age group, adapted to their needs and abilities. Adults are mentioned first, undoubtedly because of the more recent recognition of their central role.

The canon enumerates three groups whose aid the pastor is to enlist in accomplishing the ongoing catechetical task: 1) Clerics attached to the parish. 2) Religious, when the nature of their institute, its life and apostolate do not militate against such involvement. 3) Lay persons, all of whom, by virtue of their baptism and confirmation, share in the concern for deepening and developing the faith of the believing community. Among the laity, the canon singles out two groups for special mention: (a) catechists and (b) parents.

Finally, the canon urges all of the above persons to be generously co-operative when called upon to collaborate with the parish pastor in catechetical endeavours. All have an obligation – at least of support and concern – and, unless there are good reasons why they are not able to help, they should willingly assist. Naturally, in all of the above categories of potential helpers, consideration ought to be given to natural talent, aptitude, strength of faith, knowledge, training and ability in addition to willingness.

Canon 777 focuses on several pastoral situations that have particular catechetical requirements. It serves as a checklist of special times and particular groups that call for customised religious instruction. The canon does not imply that the pastor must give these instructions personally. It simply states that it is his duty to see that they are provided. Specifically with regard to adults it notes:

> In accord with the norms established by the diocesan bishop, the pastor is to make particular provision that the faith of young people and adults be fortified, enlightened and developed through various means and endeavours (Canon 775 n.5).

Canon 779 portrays a pastoral exhortation about the means to be used in the catechetical ministry, the necessary adaptation of the methods to the audience and a reminder of the goals that the ministry strives to achieve. It had no counterpart in the 1917 Code. It is, in fact, derived from the documents *Christus Dominus*[21], *Inter Mirifica*[22] and *Catechesi Tradendae*[23].

> Catechetical formation is to be given by employing all those helps, teaching aids and communications media which appear to be more effective in enabling the faithful to learn the Catholic teaching more fully and practice it more suitably in the light of their characteristics, talents and conditions of life (Canon 779).

The canon urges the use of the full panoply of the means of communication available in the modern world – television, radio, the press, records etc. Their suitability relies on their adaptation to those being reached; the canon lists four measures of the human situation of the faithful to be considered: natural disposition, abilities, age and circumstances of life. Finally, the canon states the aim of the catechetical enterprise: that believers learn the teaching of their religion more fully and reduce that teaching to practice more aptly.

The missionary activity of the Church
The second major section of Book III on the Church's teaching office sets down norms for the task most closely associated with catechesis, i.e. missionary activity. Again, it is a departure from the 1917 Code which, except for incidental references, did not consider laws governing the missions as part of the legislation for the universal Church. The revised Code makes it clear that the Church, in its very essence, is missionary and everyone in the Church has a fundamental responsibility for proclaiming the gospel to the non-evangelised.[24] The main sources for the norms in canons 781-792 are the conciliar documents *Lumen Gentium, Ad Gentes* and *Christus Dominus*.

The pope and bishops are charged in various ways with initiating, fostering and co-ordinating missionary activity.[25] Canon 786 describes missionary activity and the principal way in which it is carried out. It says that missionary activity means planting the Church among peoples and communities where it has not yet been rooted. It is accomplished chiefly by sending heralds until the Church is established, that is, until the new Church has the means to carry on the work of evangelisation by itself:

> Catechists are to be employed in carrying out missionary work; catechists are those members of the Christian faithful who have been duly instructed, who stand out by reason of their Christian manner of life and who devote themselves to expounding the gospel, teaching and organising liturgical functions and works of charity under the supervision of a missionary (Canon 785 n.1).

Although the canons do not say so explicitly, it is clear that the 'heralds' of the good news are missionaries and catechists. *Ad Gentes* 17, the principal source for this canon, recognises the importance of the catechists' role. It recommends that they should receive a canonical mission in a public liturgical celebration so as to enhance their work and official standing.

Canon 787 sees missionary activity in two stages. Firstly, missionaries, whether or not they are native to the country in which they are working,[26] are called upon to initiate dialogue with non-believers, taking into account the background and culture of the people. The next step for those judged ready to accept the gospel message, is instruction in the faith so that they may be admitted to baptism if they so desire. The task of preparing individuals for baptism presumably falls to the catechist and is undertaken in the context of the catechumenate.[27] The formation of the neophytes is to continue even after baptism.

Canon 789 calls for a formation that, more than mere instruction, engenders love for Christ and his Church. The brevity of this canon does not enable it to capture the spirit and richness of the conciliar text on which it is based. *Ad Gentes* 15, citing Ephesians 4:1, instructs missionaries to raise up 'congregations of the faithful who will walk in a manner worthy of the vocation to which they are called'.

The last two canons in this section specify ways in which local Churches are to foster missionary co-operation. Canon 791 says that every diocese should (a) promote missionary vocations, (b) designate a priest to promote activities for the benefit of the missions, especially the official papal programme, (c) celebrate an annual mission day and (d) send the Holy See a suitable sum of money annually for the support of the missions.

Canon 792 envisions communion and co-operation between the Churches. It instructs Episcopal Conferences in areas where the Church is established to promote projects that will provide a welcome and supportive reception of those who come from mission lands for the purpose of studying or working.[28]

Catholic education

After setting down some general principles, the new code legislates for formal Catholic education in three chapters: (i) 'schools' (ii) 'Catholic universities and other institutions of higher studies' and (iii) 'Ecclesiastical Universities and Faculties'. In all there are twenty-three canons (almost twice as many as in the 1917 Code; see canons 807-814), strongly reflective of Vatican II's document on Christian education, *Gravissimum Educationis*.

Symbolic of the spirit and direction of the revised code is the fact that the very first word in the section is 'parents'. Parents are said to have both the obligation and the right to educate their offspring. (The same obligation and right belongs to adoptive parents and legal guardians). Catholic parents also have the duty to see to the formation of their children in the Catholic faith in the best way open to them, and likewise they have the right to select, among those available in their area, the programmes and schools most suitable. Similarly, it is their right to claim from the state the help they need to provide for the Catholic education of their children.[29] This canon with its emphasis on the rights of parents (which are outlined but not expanded upon) is drawn from *Gravissimum Educationis*, 3, 6 and 7.

The Church's role in formal education is outlined in Canon 794. This canon grounds the Church's duty and right in its divine mission to assist people to grow into the fullness of Christian life. *Gravissimum Educationis* 3, on which this text is based claims this right also because the Church is a human society. This latter argument has value in a secular context where the divine mandate might not be recognised. The responsibility for making arrangements so that all the faithful have the benefit of a Catholic education is laid upon the pastors of souls', i.e., bishops and parish priests.

Canon 795 presents a statement on educational goals distilled from *Gravissimum Educationis* 1. It stresses four elememts: (i) Education is holistic in that it seeks the integral formation of the entire person and is concerned with the development of physical, moral, and intellectual endowments; (ii) Education is developmental as it takes into consideration the growth which children and young people experience, it fosters a sense of gradual formation, evolution of talents, and a greater sense of responsibility and use of freedom; (iii) Education is social as it aims at the common good of society, insisting on a refined sense of responsibility and right use of freedom for the well-being of the human community; (iv) Education is personal in the sense that it seeks to direct persons towards their ultimate destiny, which is life with God. The canon and its source document both merit the educator's frequent reflection.

PAUL VI AND JOHN PAUL II: UNIFORMITY AND DIVERGENCE

The catechetical vision of Pope Paul VI can be discerned from an analysis of the documents produced during his pontificate. Those concerned specifically with catechesis have already been examined. They included the *General Catechetical Directory*, the documents relating to the 1977 Synod on Catechesis as well as the 1972 *Rite of Christian Initiation of Adults*. All of the above were born out of mandates received directly from the Second Vatican Council and are fully consistent with the theological framework the Council employed.

It has been noted that catechesis in the post- conciliar era began to be understood in a newer light and in a broader perspective. Paul VI's pontificate witnessed a marked movement away from the catechism as a major (and, perhaps, sole) catechetical tool. Catechesis, under his pastoral reign, was less concerned with content (especially orthodoxy) than with methodology (who is to be catechised and how). It has been noted that the proposition relating to the compilation of a new Universal Catechism of doctrine for the whole Church was firmly rejected at the 1977 Synod under his pontificate.

As regards methodology, a renewed understanding of the practices of the early church provided a basis for late twentieth century catechesis. Thus, in the ideal vision of Paul VI, catechesis directed towards adults became the chief form to be employed. Catechesis was also to take place in the heart of the local Christian community within which every member had educational responsibilites. Above all, catechesis was to be linked to the community's commemoration of the Paschal Mystery in its annual liturgical cycle.

Although Pope John Paul II has issued considerably fewer documents on the topic (and has not had the opportunity to preside over any synod dealing directly with the catechetical mission) there is evidence to suggest that his catechetical vision differs significantly from that of his immediate predecessors – and, indeed, from the spirit of Vatican II, itself.

Much of the catechetical vision of the present pontiff can be located in his major document issued in October 1979, *Catechesis in our time*.

The document builds upon many of the existing post-conciliar insights. Firstly, one of the opening paragraphs insists on the Christocentricity of all authentic catechesis.[30] Secondly, the fact that catechesis is inextricably linked to the liturgical life of the community is stressed:

> Catechesis is intimately bound up with the whole of the Church's life (Par. 13).

and

> Catechesis is intrinsically linked with the whole of liturgical and sacramental activity, for it is in the sacraments, especially in the Eucharist, that Christ Jesus works in fullness for the transformation of human beings[31] ... catechetical teaching ... finds its source and its fulfillment in the Eucharist, within the whole circle of the liturgical year. [32]

Thirdly, John Paul II acknowledges that the entire community has a shared catechetical responsibility:

> ... catechesis always has been and always will be a work for which the whole Church must feel responsible and must wish to be responsible ... (Par. 16).

Paragraph 24 is more specific when it states

> ... the ecclesial community at all levels has a twofold responsibility with regard to catechesis. It has the responsibility of providing for the training of its members but it also has the responsibility of welcoming them into an environment where they can live as fully as possible what they have learned.

Furthermore, the 'parish community must ... be the prime mover and pre-eminent place for catechesis' (Par. 67).

John Paul also makes the point that the aim of catechesis is to develop faith as well as to advance and nourish the Christian life of the faithful, young and old.[33] Thus, he acknowledges that catechesis is a lifelong process and not just confined to children. In fact, he states that catechesis of adults:

> is the principal form of catechesis, because it is addressed to persons who have the greatest responsibilities and the capacity to live the Christian message in its fully developed form (Par. 43).

If John Paul's catechetical methodology parallels that of Paul VI with regard to the importance of catechising adults by means of communal liturgical celebrations, it diverges significantly as far as the concern for content is concerned. Throughout much of John Paul's writings there is an underlining grave concern for orthodoxy.

Knowledge of doctrine appears to be given priority over all other kinds of knowledge. In *Catechesi Tradendae* he says that catechesis is:

> ... an education of children, young people and adults in the faith which includes *especially* the teaching of Christian doctrine imparted, generally speaking, in an organic and systematic way ... [*Italics mine*] (Par. 18).

Likewise, he stresses the '... need for organic and systematic Christian instruction, because of the tendency in various quarters to minimise its importance'[34] When speaking about specific groups whose task it is to '... make Jesus known and to live by the gospel' he is equally concerned with the content of catechesis. Such groups include '... Catholic Action groups, charitable groups, prayer groups and Christian meditation groups.' He asks their leaders

> ... not to allow them [members] to lack serious study of Christian doctrine. If they do, they will be in danger – a danger that has unfortunately proved only too real – of disappointing their members and also the Church (Par. 47).

John Paul II also expressed concern about aspects of anthropological catechesis in which the Christian message is discerned and interpreted by an individual in the midst of communal life experiences:

It is quite useless to campaign for the abandonment of serious and orderly study of the message of Christ in the name of a method concentrating on life experiences (Par. 22).

In connection with memorisation of doctrinal formulae, the pope states that for such there is '... a real need'.[35] He may, thus, have paved the way for a return to the centrality of the catechism as a catechetical tool. This is given further credence by the fact that the *General Catechetical Directory* did not, in fact, abolish catechisms but made recommendations to guide the compilation of ones for local usage.[36]

The early eighties bore witness to a major turning point in the history of the catechism. Having been all but discarded twenty years previously, Rome once again began to re-examine its possible usage. In 1983 Cardinal Joseph Ratzinger, the Prefect for the Congregation for the Doctrine of the Faith stated that 'It was an initial and grave error to suppress the catechism and to declare obsolete the whole idea of catechisms'.[37] As chairman of the Commission for the Faith of the German Episcopal Conference he assigned the task of compiling a new catechism for adults to Walter Kasper of the Catholic Faculty at the University of Tübingen. The result was the production of the *Katholischer Erwachsenen-Katechismus* in 1984,[38] a text worthy of careful study (but beyond the scope of this work) because it provides important insights into the kind of catechism Cardinal Ratzinger thinks would help rescue catechesis from what many describe as its present crisis.

Undoubtedly the production of this German catechism was one of the reasons why, shortly afterwards, the 1985 Synod of Bishops (headed by John Paul II) reversed the firm decision of the bishops at the 1977 synod (headed by Paul VI). The 1977 synod had ruled out the idea of introducing a Universal Catechism. Yet, eight years later, the 1985 synod recommended:

> the compilation of a catechism or compendium of all Catholic doctrine regarding both faith and morals ... a point of reference for the catechisms or compendia that are prepared in the various regions.[39]

The scope of the synod's recommendation underwent considerable refinement from the initial proposal put forward during the first week of the 1985 synod. As summarised in the English Language edition of *L'Osservatore Romano*, the Pope urged that:

... a Commission of Cardinals [is] to prepare a draft of a Conciliar Catechism to be promulgated by the Holy Father after consulting the bishops of the world. In a shrinking world – a global village – national catechisms will not fill the current need for clear articulation of the Church's faith. [40]

A catechism emanating from so high an authority would be a departure from any previous catechism in the Catholic tradition and, indeed, a departure from the spirit if not the word of Vatican II. It would seem inevitable that such a compendium would be given the status of a confessional document like those of Heidelberg and Westminster.

In the closing address of that 1985 Synod, Pope John Paul II singled out the proposal for a 'compendium of catechism' for special mention.[41] Cardinal Ratzinger quickly established a commission to work on this Universal Catechism for the entire Roman Church.[42] This, undoubtedly, represented a major divergence from both Vatican II's and Paul VI's single vision of catechesis. Their vision sought to move away from the four hundred year old legacy of the Catechism of the Council of Trent (with its emphasis on content) towards a vision which saw doctrine (the importance of which can not be underestimated or neglected) as but one strand of a very broad catechetical spectrum.

The concept of a Universal Catechism has been the subject of much debate over the past number of years. In general, the merits pertaining to a source book of Christian doctrine being available were acknowledged. However, the predominant mood among theologians and catechists alike was that the time is not yet right (and, indeed, never will be) to undertake a mammoth task such as a codification of doctrine – primarily because doctrine is an expression of the Christian faith at a given time and within a given context. While 'the faith' cannot change, the manner in which it is expressed can and does. Realistically, then, it is a common view that a *corpus* of Christian doctrines for universal usage is not feasible.[43]

Despite adverse comments, progress on the compilation of such a master manual of doctrine continued at a steady rate. In 1989 a draft Catechism for the Universal Church[44] was sent to Episcopal Conferences around the world for a review. The Irish Episcopal Conference, at its meeting in June 1990 discussed the document.[45] The comments and recommendations relating to this project (subsequently returned to Rome) by the Irish bishops did not look favourably on the draft (mainly for theological reasons mentioned above) and included the following reservations:

1. The original desire that the catechism should present doctrine in a manner accommodated to the life of the Church today is not sufficiently met.

2. The view of the Church which appears throughout the draft is lacking the richness of the vision of Vatican II.

3. The text lacks historical, cultural and experimenatal contact with the contemporary 'signs of the times'.

4. Faith as obedience is well presented but [not] ... as the basis of a personal relationship with God.

5. The priorities and emphases of Vatican II are not followed.

6. The focus on people and on *koinonia* found in the second Vatican Council is missing.

7. The paragraphs on baptism fail to capture the spirit, the journey of conversion and the communal sponsorship of the catechumen as it is found in the R.C.I.A.

8. There is ... a lack of a sense of relationship between liturgy and life.

The bishops tactfully concluded that 'Whatever is finally produced should be worthy of its purpose and should be able to stand up to critical examination. It does not seem possible that this can be done without considerable further revision [of the present text]'. Thus, it seems that if the Universal Catechism is to be 'worthy of its purpose' – i.e. to offer a *corpus* of doctrine for all peoples in all places and for all times – it would appear that that purpose is not realistically attainable.

Despite the reservations listed above (and the many more from other National Conferences of Bishops worldwide) a final text in Latin (not too dissimilar from the draft copy circulated in 1989) was issued from Rome in late 1992, with translations into the vernacular following later.

POST-CONCILIAR PERSPECTIVES ON FAITH DEVELOPMENT:

CONCLUSIONS

Having examined in some detail the major post-conciliar documents relating to catechesis, the following conclusions can be drawn from their content.

1. Adult catechesis is to be considered the chief form of catechesis.

2. All other forms of catechesis are subordinate to (but directed towards) adult catechesis.

3. The model of catechesis favoured in post-conciliar thought is that of initiation into the adult Christian way of life.

4. The process of catechetical initiation into this Christian life is one which takes place in the midst of the existing faith community.

5. All members of the Christian community share the responsibility for such initiation.

6. In initiating new members into the Christian life, the community itself has its own faith deepened and renewed in the process.

7. Catechesis is a multi-dimensional on-going process which ought to be linked and accommodated to the annual commemoration and re-enactment of the Paschal Mystery.

8. The R.C.I.A. is both theologically and catechetically normative.

CHAPTER V

Faith development in the light of Vatican II:
IRISH POLICY AND ACTION

INTRODUCTION

The previous chapters outlined a renewed model of catechesis as presented in the conciliar (and later developed in post-conciliar) documents. That model saw catechesis primarily as a process of initiation into an adult faith community. It was also acknowledged that catechesis ought to be accommodated to the liturgical celebration of the Paschal Mystery in the annual Church cycle of events. All other forms of catechesis (including those related to the formative years of childhood and youth) are presented as being subordinate to adult faith development.

The final part of this book examines how the Irish Church has, over the past three decades, incorporated the insights and recommendations of Vatican II in relation to catechesis.

In this chapter, I will attempt to examine the felt needs of adult catechesis in Ireland at present, to trace its development and, thirdly, to identify current policy and action on the part of the Irish bishops in this area.

THE PRESENT SITUATION IN ADULT EDUCATION

The value a society places on adult catechesis and faith development will, by and large, be related to the value placed on the broader concept of adult education itself. Thus, any work which relates to the necessity and desirability, as well as to the weaknesses and strengths, of contemporary adult catechesis must assess the contemporary understanding of the value of (and the provision made for) adult education.

To achieve this it will suffice to refer briefly to some important sociological surveys concerned with participation in, and perception of, continuing adult education. It will also be of benefit, and therefore desirable, that official government policy on the subject be examined.

Attitudes towards adult education

Over the past decade a good deal of attention has been shown to the area of adult/continuing education. Surveys have shown that the Irish population has, by and large, become more aware of the need for, and the value of, this type of education. This can be seen from the survey conducted by the Working Party established by the Adult Education Commission, *Adults and Education: A Survey 1982-1983*.[1]

This comprehensive survey examined, among other aspects, the relationship between people's past experiences of involvement in formal structured education and their present view of the value of adult/continuing eduction.

With regard to the value of formal education for its own sake the survey outlined that:

> ... more women ... and middle class groups are more likely to agree that education is important for its own sake than working class persons; and more of those over 44 years of age and in the self-employed [groups] than in other groups. Those who stayed in school beyond the age of compulsory attendance were more inclined to stress the importance of education for its own sake, and the value to themselves of self-improvement. [2]

The attitude towards formal education is also somewhat reflected in the value placed by Irish society upon adult/continuing education. It can be argued that those who enjoyed formal structured education, who remained in school beyond the age of compulsory education and who saw the value of it in their lives, were more inclined to value the merits of adult/continuing education than those who had opposite experiences and feelings in the past. This is also relflected in the 1982-83 survey:

> Thus, insofar as there is a general image of adult classes, they are seen to appeal to the young more than the middle-aged or old, to the middle class rather than the working class, to office workers rather than factory or farm workers ... [3]

However, it would be incorrect to suggest that the image of those who participate in such ongoing educational endeavours is quite so simplistic. It is, in fact, rather more complex than it is often assumed to be. Adult educators have often alleged that the general public see adult education as largely an activity of the middle-aged, the middle classes and especially of women. In fact, what emerges from the above survey is that those who are young, urban dwellers, single persons, women, office workers, middle class and those seeking to improve their position are thought to be those most likely to attend. The statistics relating to actual participation (which will now be looked at) indicate otherwise.

Participation in adult education courses
The most recent statistics available on participation in adult/continuing education comes from the survey conducted by Micheál Mac Gréil (during the period from November 1988-April 1989) and published by the Survey and Research Unit at the Department of Social Studies, St Patrick's College, Maynooth in 1990.

The findings give a profile of those who stated that they have attended adult/continuing education courses since leaving school. The age group 18-50 years were significantly higher in number than those 51 years and over in the proportion attending such courses.

The slightly higher [+4.5%] proportion of females than males who have reported attending adult education courses is in line with the overall trend of greater female participation in education. Mac Gréil comments that this may be due to choice of curriculum and available facilities, eg., women's studies, fashion and design etc. [4]

The findings by area of residence are interesting and possibly reflect the greater opportunities available in urban areas. This is borne out especially in relation to Connaught/Ulster where the level of participation is substantially lower than in any of the other provinces.

One of the most interesting positive links in Mac Gréil's study relates the variables of level of formal education attained to participation in adult/continuing education. A similar link exists in relation to occupational status. 'Blue-collar' and lesser educated sub-samples have a substantially lower participation rate to date.

The findings indicate that the respondents' evaluation of their experiences of adult education is, apparently, based upon its perceived relevance and usefulness for their lives and careers. This fact is, obviously, of great significance to Adult Religious Educators. Mac Gréil comments that:

> There is a marked absence of emphasis on courses in the area of religion, philosophy, culture and purely educational subjects.

This may be due to the limitation of the range of courses offered or the easy access to them.[5]

This may be true. But it is also possible that these courses may not have been seen as desirable or relevant by either the participants in or providers of such courses.

Government policy on adult education

A general consensus on what the aims of education are seems, in the past, to have existed unchallenged within the state. Such aims have been reflected, for instance, in formal and informal statements by professionl educationalists, community leaders and Ministers for Education, in educationl publications and in official documents such as *Curaclaim na Bunscoile*, 1971;[6] *Rules and Programme for Secondary Schools*, 1972;[7] the *White Paper on Educational Development*, 1980;[8] and the *Programme for Action in Eduction*, 1984.[9] These have all located education within the classroom and saw it as concerned chiefly with minors.

In relation to adult education, the first serious attempt to examine the whole issue took place in 1969. Firstly, there was the setting up of *Aontas*, a broadly representative national voluntary body of adult educators acting in a consultative capacity for the government.

Later, in May of that year, the Minister for Education appointed Con Murphy to carry out a 'survey of the needs of the community in the matter of adult education, and to indicate the type of permanent organisation to be set up in order to serve those needs'. To help in this task an advisory committee of ten was also appointed.

An Interim Report was issued by Murphy in 1971.[10] This document defined adult education as 'all the educational activity engaged in by people who have broken with full-time continuous education'. One of the recommendations of the report was the setting up of a council for adult education at national level to consist of eleven members who, in turn, would be responsible to a chief executive. In trying to co-ordinate adult education on a national level the recommendations seem to be at variance with the basic concept of adult education as a person-centred, learning, need-solving activity related to the local community.

The final report, *Adult Education in Ireland*,[11] was presented to the Minister in November 1973. It outlined a healthy participation in adult education already existing – approximately ten per cent of the adult population participated in formal classes and about the same proportion in adult training, in in-service and retraining programmes. It was considered that an unknown (but probably equal) percentage of the adult population participated in 'non-formal adult education'. This would indicate that (if true), as far back as 1973, a section as high as thirty per cent of the adult population were taking advantage of educational opportunities available to them. This seems highly unlikely as Mac Gréil's most recent study shows that the only subgroups to have such a high level of participation in adult education are higher executives and those who have already gained a third level education.[12]

Another finding of the Committee was that, in general, those participating were in the 21 to 45 years age group, had at least two years of post-primary education and were members of the upper socio-economic groups. Males tended to avail of courses related to their occupations and females of courses related to domestic roles.

Some of the recommendations of the 1973 report were quite novel. The Committee, for example, saw the realisation of 'permanent education' as necessitating a 'complete change, indeed a revolution, in the present Irish system of education'. Amongst other things they considered that such a change should inevitably lead to the 'end of learning by rote, which is the assembly and memorising of facts, pieces of information etc.,' and instead secure 'a discernment on where and how to secure, utilise and integrate knowledge'.[13]

Seven years later saw the publication of the White Paper on Educational Development [1980]: *Adult Education*.[14] Here the government of the day indicated its intention to promote and develop adult education 'as circumstances permitted'. It acknowledged that special consideration should be given to the needs of the disadvantaged, the illiterate and those wishing to avail of second-chance education.

A year later the Minister for Education announced the establishment of an advisory body to prepare a national development plan for adult and continuing education. This advisory body, the Commission on Adult Education, as it was called, worked between November 1981 and May 1983 to produce its report *Lifelong Learning: Report of the Commission on Adult Education*.[15] This latter document is, undoubtedly the most significant to date on the subject and, although it may not reflect actual government policy, it does draw up concrete proposals for government action. Thus, it merits examination in some detail.

The working definition of adult education employed throughout by the Commission was as follows:

> Adult Education includes all systematic learning by adults which contributes to their development as individuals and as members of the community and of society apart from full-time instruction received by persons as part of their uninterrupted initial education and training. It may be formal education which takes place in institutions e.g. training centres, schools, colleges, institutes and universities; or non-formal education, which is any other systematic form of learning, including self-directed learning.[16]

The great significance attributed to adult/continuing education by the Commission can be determined from the very first paragraph of the report which put forward the view that 'at this time of rapid change, adult education is not a luxury but is essential'. It is the 'versatile and ubiquitous agent for democratizing the cultural heritage of the people and facilitating their further personal development in all seasons'. From the point of view of advantage to the State the report outlined that:

> adult education can provide an important stimulus to the more systematic acquisition of knowledge about problems in Europe and in the world at large ... A well informed and educated public which is capable of influencing policy formation will not only contribute to the soundness of international policies and commitments but will sustain the vitality of democracy at home.[17]

The Commission acknowledged that there is a wide range in the present provision of adult education in Ireland. Adult education has grown in response to the needs and problems of society. Having recognised particular needs and problems, people have often come together to tackle them in voluntary groups. Some of these groups have received a measure of government recognition and support. The most notable aspect in the provision of all such statutory and voluntary education, however, is that it has grown without a coherent national plan.

The Commission listed several agencies and institutions at

present employed in adult / continuing education. These included the Vocational Education System, Community and Comprehensive Schools, Voluntary Secondary Schools, Universities, Colleges of Industrial Relations, Management and Administrative Institutes, R.T.É., ACOT, Training Agencies for the Handicapped, Trade Unions, as well as Public Libraries, Museums, Galleries etc.

Attention is drawn to the fact that in the Deed of Trust for Community Schools it is specified that such schools:

> would provide adult education facilities in the area and ... would make facilities available to voluntary organisations and to the adult community generally. As there are now more than fifty such schools they have begun to constitute a significant part of the adult education service. As originally intended many of them have developed into community learning centres, which attract large numbers of adults and are the focus of many formal and non-formal educational activities.[18]

The Commission concluded that there exists a lack of awareness and considerable misunderstanding about adult education – what it is, who provides it, who goes to classes and where to obtain information about it. To overcome these and other perceived problems the Commission outlined comprehensive details on how adult/continuing education could be organised and co-ordinated at both national and local level.

The Curriculum and Examinations Board, in its September 1984 document, *Issues and Structures in Education: A Consultative Document*,[19] also strongly outlined the need for life-long education. It suggested that it is no longer easy to demarcate particular areas of educationl competence properly only to the home, or to the community, or to the school. Rather:

> ... education is now seen as a continuous, shared process, in which all three participate and must co-operate. Nor is it possible today – if ever it really was possible – to identify a terminal point at which a person's education, even in a more or less formal sense, is 'complete'. The various levels in a system are now seen as related stages in recurrent, and indeed, permanent, life-long education.[20]

It would be very inaccurate to suggest that actual government policy in the past two decades (as far as it is possible to discern such) is consistent in its recognition of the value and importance it attributes to life-long education. It is permissible to expect diverging and opposing opinions on the matter from different governments of the day. However, individaul Education Ministers have, at times in the same document, offered conflicting views on the matter. One example of this is to be found in the 1984 *Programme for Action in Education*.

Here the Minister acknowledges the desirability of 'continuing education' for all citizens partly because education is about, among other things, the transmission of a value system'. However, a major (if not principal) aim of education in this document is presented mainly as securing employment. Consequently the educational system must change with changing employment patterns especially with reference to curriculum development.[21] Thus, inevitably, technology becomes a chief guiding principle for educational developments[22] – which is somewhat inconsistent with most contemporary models of education.

In a detailed response to the document, one third level academic establishment summed up that the economic priorities evident in the text suggest:

> ... a consumer model which understands education in terms of meeting the demands of the market place and which leads inevitably to speaking of education in terms of productivity and cost-efficiency.[23]

Of equal interest is the fact that the document is largely silent on the subject of religious education, either in the formal curriculum or in relation to life-long learning. Thus, the Minister neglects the educational requirements already presupposed in par. 1.10 of the same document: 'there should be development of all the individuals qualities – spiritual, moral, intellectual, aesthetic and physical'. This is, undoubtedly, a serious lacuna in a document the importance of which is reflected in its title: *Programme for Action in Education 1984-1987*.

The introduction to the most recent government document on educaution, the *Green Paper on Education* 1992, issued on April 20th, devotes relatively little attention to adult education. It affirms the '... need to develop students for life as well as for work' and also acknowledges the need '... to provide increasingly for "second chance" education'. Such provision, it is envisaged, would involve the opening up of vocational training programmes to adults and the '... expanded involvement of all secondary schools in extended programmes of adult education'. The introduction also recommends that access to third-level education for mature students should be further developed and adult literacy programmes ought to be expanded. The very nature of the introduction to the Green Paper, as a discussion document, leaves one with the impression that, although the importance of adult education is acknowledged, the treatment it receives lacks both careful thought and planning. As such, it is best to look upon the paper's allusion to adult education as a beginning rather than as an end in itself.

ADULT CATECHESIS IN IRELAND: THE PRESENT STATUS

It has already been noted that the State has, for some time now, shown considerable interest in the area of adult education and has taken modest steps towards providing for its expansion. Although restrained by financial cutbacks, it does, indeed, acknowledge the value of life-long and continuing education. Such an acknowledgement is of the greatest significance in that it provides a starting point for further co-ordinated policy and action in the future.

The growth in the area of adult catechesis in Ireland since the Second Vatican Council has, in comparison, been a slow and haphazard one. Unlike the State, the Irish Episcopal Conference appears to have offered little or no official indication of the need for adults to be involved in organised lifelong, continuing education in (and development of) their faith – apart from an all too brief Mulranny Statement.[24] Thus, religious education continues to relate mainly to, and be centred in, primary and second level schools. Questions have already been asked (in Chapter I) whether or not the Irish Church is devoting too much of its educational resources to primary and secondary level schooling at the expense of other equally important sections of the Christian community, especially the adult community.

Early stages in the evolution of adult religious education
Without an official awareness of the need for lifelong adult religious education and without a co-ordinated approach from the Irish Episcopal Conference (the Conference never discussed it in any significant depth), the growth in this area has, as a result, been largely at the discretion of individual bishops in their respective dioceses.

With that in mind, I will now attempt to formulate an accurate picture of the efforts that have been undertaken to date to provide for adult religious education. In order to achieve this it is neither desirable nor necessary to present a comprehensive account of all the projects which have been undertaken in this country since 1962 in the name of adult religious education. Rather, it will prove more beneficial, in this section, to draw attention to different approaches to adult religious education which have been employed and into which all past and present efforts fall.

Local community providing for adult religious education
Many of the adventures into adult religious education, in the past, have come about largely as a result of communities recognising the need for further / ongoing education in career-related areas of life and later discerning a need also for religious education. A good example of this was Limerick's Adult Education Centre. As early as 1966 a group of local people felt that, given the Irish 'passion for education', there were areas of learning that existing institutions did not cater for, and that if courses were offered through an autonomous and self-supporting organisation people would come and attend the classes. This, in fact, proved to be the case.[25]

The Adult Education Centre which resulted experienced some considerable changes during its initial years in existence. As local educational needs became apparent some of the classes on the original curriculum were dropped while new ones were added. One of the areas of felt need was that of theology and religious studies. These classes were successfully provided for in an ecumenical environment by a Jesuit priest, a Franciscan friar and a Methodist minister.

One point of particular interest in relation to the Limerick Adult Education Centre was that it was not in receipt of financial support from any State or Church agencies. This did, in fact, prove to be problematical in that courses which failed to attract sufficient students in the first year to make them self-supporting had to be dropped. It also contributed to the fact that fees were higher than they might have been and thus less accessible to some members of the community.

Church providing for adult religious education
A second more interesting development in the field of adult religious education can be seen with regard to Kilkenny's Adult Education Centre. Here the Church (in the form of the local bishop)

helped establish a centre for adult education in 1974. The centre's chief aim was to provide for the educational needs of local adults. Interestingly enough, neither theology nor religious studies were included until a later period in the life of the centre.

Bishop Birch, in deciding to purchase an empty local convent, saw the educational possibilities it presented:

> We needed a workshop for mentally handicapped adults and we needed a home and a school for emotionally disturbed children. As well as that, it was very obvious that we needed a centre for adult education. We thought it would serve as part of the education of adults to see these other activities taking place near by, so that there was no conflict between the various parts of the work. The project was conceived as a community one and was pushed forward as a community one.[26]

The bishop's experiences led him to believe that during times when convents and schools are being closed, none ought to go out of community use, and if possible not out of educational use – 'we cannot afford this waste'.

Again, it took some years for the centre to identify its needs. Relying, for the most part, on course fees to cover expenses meant that subjects of interest and benefit to the local community had to be carefully chosen. However, if a group were genuinely interested in a particular subject a course was put on for them, even if the group was small and financially not able to support itself.

The centre was used for adult community education in the broadest sense possible. It offered courses on a diverse range of subjects of local interest: modern literature, design and manufacture, commerce and politics as well as making parents aware of what their children were studying in school. As already noted, only later were courses of a religious nature made available. The centre was also used as a venue for the continuing education of priests and religious. This was made possible by using the resources of priests within the diocese who were qualified in theology, scripture, liturgy, catechetics and social studies.

Perhaps the main reason why courses were not offered in religious studies initially was due to problems with motivation. According to Birch, it is not easy to overcome the natural inertia of people who have settled into life: motivation has to be strong and properly directed to get them to take a course.[27] Worthwhile certification was seen as one possible approach to enhance motivation. However, Birch and most of the adults who attended, saw the idea of a college devoted mainly to general and religous studies as, in fact, 'not a luxury, but an absolute necessity'.[28]

The basic needs of adult religious education emerge
In his 1977 critique of adult religious education in Ireland, Liam Carey was able to say 'Adult Religious Education does not exist in Ireland. There are, as yet, no clearly defined structures of adult religious education'.[29] Other educationalists familiar with this field agree with him. For example, Joseph McCann noted that

> ... there is a serious lack of direction and impact in Adult Religious Education in Ireland. Usually this is described as a lack of co-ordination or leadership ... Co-ordination and leadership differ; one kind is required to keep existing arrangements going, quite another variety is called for when the task is to create something where nothing exists as yet ... There seems to be no national structures at all intended to investigate or support parish catechetical programmes, or Adult Religious Education.[30]

Carey, for his part, identified Adult Religious Education in Ireland to date [1977] as having taken the following form:[31]

(a) Short courses for parents, e.g., parents of First Communicants, or parents of children who are being confirmed.

(b) Pre-marriage courses and some post-marriage courses.

(c) Family Group Movements.

(d) Bible Study and Prayer Groups.

(e) Planned Group/Family Masses.

(f) Planned set of Patrician Meetings.

(g) Formation programmes for some lay-apostolate organisations.

(h) Christian encounter groups.

(i) Some family Life Programmes, e.g. Child Development.

(j) Many small *ad hoc* groups who come together for a period of time to examine some aspect of the Christian faith and its application to their own real world.

(k) Retreats of various types and forms.

Liam Lacey acknowledges that such models for adult catechesis have been very helpful in leading people to a better understanding of their religion.[32] They have contributed much in assisting adults towards deepening their faith. He suggests, however, that their primary limitation lies in their lack of a guiding principle or focus for action.

Carey in 1981 outlined the objectives of Adult Religious Education as follows:[33]

* to help the adult grow to maturity in the Christian faith.

* to enable the adult realise what are his or her responsibilities in the Catholic Church, the parish or basic Christian community.

* to encourage the adult to fulfil his or her roles and functions as a member of a Christian community.

* to stimulate the adult to engage in building and forming the Christian community of justice, truth, love and freedom.

* to help the adult integrate Christian principles into the socio-economic and cultural life of his/her family, community and country.

* to develop in the adult a readiness and a willingness to engage in community service and action in relation to the needy, e.g. the poor, the unemployed, the lonely, the elderly, the aged, the traveller, the disadvantaged, etc.

* to create in the adult, enthusiasm and a keeness to expand his/her understanding of the comprehensive Christian message and to discover the origin and the basis of that message.

* to enable the adult to cope with and understand change, which affects Christian living, worship and service in a rapidly changing technological society.

Carey's list of the aims of adult religious education is comprehensive and his critique of the situation in 1977 appears quite accurate, yet one still remains devoid of a methodology to advance the attainment of those aims within the Irish context.

Contemporary adult religious education programmes
According to a contemporary educationalist, one of the main reasons why much of the dynamic theology of Vatican II has not been implemented at parish level is that it is not accompanied by

an equally dynamic programme of adult religious education for both clergy and laity. Thus, it can be argued, the theology of Vatican II was superimposed on a people who saw no need for it. They were not educated to see the need for change or encouraged to get involved in the process of change itself.[34]

Irish society itself has changed dramatically since the early sixties and, as a result, the Irish Church needs to provide meaningful programmes of religious learning if it is to facilitate growth towards mature, personally convinced faith in its members. Such religious learning ought to be lifelong if it is to be effective in a society like the one in contemporary Ireland where the pace of change is accelerating all the time.

In beginning to recognise this situation most Irish dioceses have, at this stage, already organised formal programmes in adult religious studies. Such programmes open up the field of theology and make it readily available, for the first time, to the public at large. Nearly all such programmes have been set up in conjunction with St Patrick's College, Maynooth which awards an Extra Mural Diploma to successful candidates. The Irish bishops have devoted a great deal of support in terms of finance and resources to such courses.

First impressions of these programmes suggest that they are successful in introducing large numbers of adults to a greater maturation of their faith and, particularly, to the contemporary theology of Vatican II. The topics dealt with include faith as a pilgrim journey, introduction to scripture, sacramental and moral theology as well as prayer and spirituality.

However, even a superficial examination of the programmes reveal many causes for concern. The first two-year religious studies programme in the Diocese of Derry (begun in September 1985) was the subject of an indepth analysis by a postgraduate student in the Department of Adult and Continuing Education in the University of Ulster at Magee College.[35]

Peter Boucher's findings prove interesting. Although they are based on one local case study, the results are in line with suspicions held by a growing number of educators about the effectiveness (and efficiency) of such university extra-mural courses.

Boucher revealed that the vast majority of the people who attended the two year programme were women [74%]. 56% of the candidates were in the age group 30-50 years of age. Perhaps most interesting of all was the fact that the majority were middle class [55%], married [60%] with third level education [45%].

Undoubtedly, such extra mural courses are of significant benefit to the people who attend. However, sociological surveys already referred to (*cf* Chapter I) would indicate that the people who attend are those least in need of assistance in the area of faith development. Mac Gréil *et al.* have, as noted, identified the problem category to be (as far as fall-off in formal religious practice is concerned) young middle aged [21-35 year olds], unskilled, single males with low educational achievements. No matter how well meaning the endeavour may be these are hardly the people who are going to be reached and helped by extra-mural courses from a third level institute.

It seems that the courses are instructional and content-centred (theology and doctrine) rather than experiential and person-centred (faith development accommodated to liturgical celebration). Thus, the approach (worthwhile on its own) is not the one consistent with either the vision of Vatican II or contemporary adult educational theory.[36] Therefore, extra mural courses in religious studies can only be looked upon as a small part (and certainly not as the end) of a process of awakening and deepening the faith of the adult Christian community.

From adult religious education to adult catechesis
The idea of adult religious education being connected to the life of the parish was one which was particularly slow to emerge in this country, although such was central to the vision of Vatican II in its conciliar and post-conciliar documents (as already noted in Chapters II-IV). Vatican II saw the ongoing education in faith of adult Christians as a pastoral priority of the Christian community at large, to be carried out in the midst of a local faith community chiefly through the celebration of its sacramental life – not removed from it, as the early attempts at adult religious education in this country tended to be. Thus, the Council preferred to speak of catechesis rather than religious education.

It must be acknowledged that for most adult Catholics the total learning environment in which catechesis takes place is the parish. All of parish life is educative for good or ill: the quality of the liturgy; the degree of involvement in shared decision-making; the priorities latent in the parish budget; the degree of commitment to social justice; the vitality of parish organisations. All of these either reward or retard a person's growth in faith and service. They all contribute to a climate which encourages persons to learn and develop or to become complacent and stagnate.

The Dublin Institute of Adult Education was one of the first bodies to move towards this logical (and crucial) connection between adult religious education and parish life. In January 1980 they appointed a committee whose objective was to 'assist Christian development at the personal and community levels'.[37] The institute acknowledged that there are many different occasions for informal adult education connected with personal, family, social and ecclesial life but there was, nevertheless, a need for organic and systematic religious education for adults. This, according to the Institute, could best be achieved in the heart of the parish itself. Thus, one of the practical means of pursuing their objective was the development of a service to parishes in the field of adult catechesis.

The idea envisaged by the Institute was to work in conjunction with any parish organistion or committee who sought their advise by utilising whatever resources (in terms of competent and qualified personnel) might be available in the parish itself.

The courses were designed to meet the specific needs of the individual parishes. For example, some of the newer parishes with a large percentage of young families, often opted for courses on 'marriage and family life' or 'moral questions today', while some of the more settled parishes showed a preference for 'understanding and praying the bible' or 'understanding our faith'. Another type of programme requested by parishes was one which related directly to the seasons of the liturgical year, especially Advent and Lent. Again, some programmes were directed towards young adults and their particular questions.[38]

In the academic year 1980-81, thirty-two courses were held in seventeen Dublin parishes. The following year twenty-six parishes requested help from the Institute. Today the Institute is one of the most successful of those involved in organised adult catechesis at parish level.

Towards a communal adult catechesis
The content of the courses offered in parishes and brought about by the involvement of the Dublin Institute of Adult Education was fairly flexible and open-ended. Having said this, however,

there does seem to be a pattern emerging which appears to point towards the planning of an overall programme of adult catechesis that covers the essential elements of Christian life. These are defined in John Paul II's *Catechesi Tradendae* as:

(a) ... the initial proclamation of the gospel to arouse faith

(b) apologetics or examination of the reasons for belief

(c) experience of Christian living

(d) celebration of the sacraments

(e) an integration into the ecclesial community

(f) apostolic and missionary witness.

A good example of such elements of Christian living being taken fully into account when planning an adult catechetical programme is the Wim Saris approach to catechesis at parish level. This programme has been used successfully in the Irish context andI will now outline it in brief.

Wim Saris approach to catechesis at parish level: Ballinteer
With the virtual abandonment of the catechism after Vatican II the approach which replaced it began to make different demands. In the past, knowledge was all important. Now the approach seemed to be more on giving personal witness to one's faith and in doing so building up the pilgrim people of God (Vatican II's preferred model of Church). Now it is the responsibility of the baptised to create conditions favourable for the living out of gospel values. In other words, it is no longer the priest or the school who have the sole responsibility for evangelisation and catechesis. The school, then, no longer ought to hold a monopoly on Catholic religious education. Thus, teamwork becomes the key to the 'new' catechetical approach. This is the basis and understanding of the Wim Saris approach to catechesis.[39]

For Saris, education occurs through people interacting. Old and young educate each other. Education is a process of growth and development of all who are involved in this symbiotic relationship. Catechesis is the same kind of relationship occurrence. He identifies four partners involved in the process: the family, the Church, the school and young people.

Saris begins with an acknowledgement that the school has been for too long the centre of catechesis. New ways must be discovered and this involves planning. He prefers not to use the term 'adult catechesis' as this would imply exclusively adults. He opts for the term 'family catechesis' because it has, as its foundation, the home. He lists four aims of family catechesis:

* to equip parents to give religious instruction in their homes. This emerges not only from their own commitment to the faith but also by giving witness to their faith at local level.

* to create an awareness of community.

* to bring about co-operation and division of labour among the parish, school and family in the area of catechesis of youth.

* to establish a directed pastoral process which will lead to the setting up of teams of laity who will be prepared to be involved in various ministries.

The Wim Saris approach has already been utilised in Ireland. Perhaps the earliest use of the programme was in the south side of Dublin city. During the summer months of 1983 priests from Dundrum, Meadowbrook and Ballinteer met with a view to setting up a catechetical programme for adults. The result was a parish programme with the theme 'Building up the People of God'.

The programme ran every Monday evening from October to March. The aim of the programme was to bring people to an awareness of their role as priests, religious and laity and to create conditions for the fulfilment of these roles. The course created an awareness of the importance of teamwork not only within the parish but also with neighbouring parishes. One of the priests involved noted:

> The importance of getting people involved in building up an awareness of themselves [means] people can no longer be confined to activities such as sales of work ... People are now looking for opportunities for involvement in the apostolate. They are agents for evangelisation and a climate must be created at local level where they can exercise their God-given right to be ministers of faith.[40]

The Wim Saris approach proved both workable and successful. Based, as it was, on a realistic catechesis, it gave rise to a vibrant local community with a unique sense of Christian identity.

The catechetical approach of the Wim Saris project differs from ones already referred to above in that this approach begins explicitly with the experience of everyday life and not from pre-set pet areas or topics for discussion. That is not to say, however, that it is without need of any input to motivate people to begin to explore what their faith means in the context of their home and their local community.

Towards a communal liturgical adult catechesis
The newer approaches to adult catechesis in Ireland examined so far have, in one way or another, looked upon catechesis as an entity which stands on its own. The Wim Saris approach acknowledged that adult catechesis ideally must be centred within a communal setting. However, adult catechesis still remained largely unconnected with the celebration of the sacraments.

The 1972 Rite of Christian Initiation of Adults (R.C.I.A.) in action
One of the first Irish parishes to attempt to accommodate adult catechesis to the communal celebration of the sacraments was St Michael's Parish in Inchicore, Dublin – a parish run by the Oblate Fathers (not diocesan clergy!). Here the model of the R.C.I.A. was successfully adapted, firstly to the parish confirmation programme and secondly to a baptismal preparation process.

The then parish priest of Inchicore became very aware of the problems a large urban parish must overcome in order to be successful in cultivating a genuine faith community. He saw his parish community as having many things in common with early Christian communities. In the past the Christian community was small in comparison to the pagan world. Today a large city parish is small in comparison to a greater secular society.

In 1982 he became aware of the possibility of the adaptation of the R.C.I.A. to the sacramental life of a parish. Seeing baptism, confirmation and eucharist as part of a rite of initiation into the Adult Christian Church he undertook to adapt the rite to the catechesis of children in the case of confirmation and towards the catechesis of parents in the case of baptism and eucharist. A full-time parish catechist was employed to co-ordinate the programme.

In this case the task of the parish catechist was well defined. The duties included:

* organising family catechesis structured around baptismal, first communion and confirmation programmes.

* building up the confidence of parents as the first and most effective teachers of their own children.

* drawing out an awareness of personal God-given gifts, uniqueness and talents in people.

* encouraging people to become more fully aware of themselves as part of a Christian community.

* endeavouring to strengthen and co-ordinate school, parish and home relations and experiences.

In the case of infant baptism, the parents and sponsors became fully involved with the preparation for the sacrament and were made fully aware of what they were undertaking. For confirmation, adults in the parish were encouraged to act as 'Faith Friends' to those who were preparing to receive the sacrament. The 'Faith Friend' approach was based largely upon the R.C.I.A. role of sponsor. Their main task was to give witness and help deepen the candidate's own faith experiences. This achieved the desired effect of having many people in the parish involved with preparation for the sacrament. Those involved found they had to question (and consequently deepen) their own faith more than they would otherwise have done.

The school's role was to strengthen the candidate's doctrinal knowledge and help link it to the faith experiences of the community at large with which they came into contact more and more.

Through preparation for the sacraments of initiation, the entire parish became involved and were made acutely aware of their parish as an initiating community. The need to have a strong faith community, worthy of initiating their children into, became very apparent.

Today the Inchicore parish continues successful adaptation of the R.C.I.A. in ways that are best suited to its own particular situation.

One of the first Irish dioceses to attempt to use the norm of the R.C.I.A. (i.e. without adaptation) was the Diocese of Ossory. Here, in the parish of Clogh, the rite was used to initiate an unbaptised adult into the Catholic Church. Under Church law, the restored catechumenal process is mandatory for such circumstances and may not be dispensed with. The candidate entered the Period of the Catechumenate in January 1984. The Stage of Illumination and Enlightenment was entered into on the first Sunday of Lent 1985. On successful completion of this stage, the candidate was baptised and confirmed during the Easter Vigil by the priest in charge of the programme. Later, during the Vigil Mass, the candidate received communion for the first time.

Here, again, the parish community was made keenly aware of their identity as an initiating faith community. However, it was not possible to involve the parish as actively as might have been desired – certainly parishioners were not as involved as those of Inchicore were in initiating minors into the sacraments of baptism, confirmation and eucharist. This is understandable, possibly because the parish may not yet have felt the need to accept responsibility to catechise others apart from their own children.

It would seem, then, that the adaptation of the R.C.I.A. for use with children offers the best method of catechesis for an entire parish. Here the dichotomy of adult catechesis *versus* minor catechesis is answered by changing the emphasis from 'either/or' to 'both/and'.

Where the future of adult catechesis lies
The 1985 *Directory of Adult Religious Education in Ireland* (the first and only year it was published)[41] lists over five hundred courses on offer. The number appears encouraging until the courses are examined in closer detail. Listings in the directory range from Drug Awareness Groups to Lenten Theology courses. It is clearly evident that most of the entries fall into the first two of the categories mentioned above i.e. (a) the local community and (b) the Church providing for adult religious education – note not adult catechesis.

However, in the years since the compilation of that directory evidence suggests that the latter two approaches have found favour i.e. the family catechesis approach of Wim Saris and the R.C.I.A. Contemporary thought is turning towards such diverse enterprises as Adult Biblical Education,[42] Parish Cells,[43] full-time parish catechists,[44] the lay ministry of hospital chaplaincy,[45] as well as the broader vocation and mission of the lay faithful.

The different approaches to adult religious education outlined above have been presented in evolutionary fashion. The first saw adult religious education under the banner of doctrinal knowledge on a par with other adult education subjects like art and design. It was undertaken out of academic interest or religious curiosity. The second approach was identical, only this time a Church structure helped organise the programme and then only when it became obvious that a demand existed for it. The Wim Saris approach placed emphasis upon communal experience as a starting point not just for adult but family catechesis. Finally, the R.C.I.A. located catechesis in the midst of a community celebrating its sacraments – even though those preparing to receive the sacraments were not adults but children and minors. It would seem that, in the Irish context, this appears to be the best approach to communal catechesis at parish level. This point will be returned to and elaborated upon later.

AWARENESS OF THE IRISH HIERARCHY
TO THE NECESSITY OF ADULT CATECHESIS

One ought, at this stage, ask how aware are the Irish bishops of the insights and recommendations of Vatican II in relation to the area of adult faith development and catechesis. Here, I will attempt to answer that question by reference to content analysis of all available pastoral letters, writings and statements issued by Irish bishops over the past three decades.

If one examines the themes treated in bishops' pastoral letters since Vatican II, one can discern the topics which appear of most importance to the Irish Episcopacy. The themes which one would expect to appear do, in fact, receive special treatment. The Mass,[46] Penance,[47] and Marriage[48] are among those most frequently treated. In short, the sacraments are the primary focus of attention in the writings of the bishops. But even here it is noticable how the treatment of these topics has changed over the past thirty years. The catechism approach to catechetical instruction, at the end of its era in the sixties,[49] gave way to instruction which was related more to pastoral than doctrinal issues.

However, it would be wrong to conclude that teaching on the sacraments and doctrinal precepts are the only matters which Irish bishops focus upon. A preliminary glance at the large amount of literature involved here indicates a wealth of rich insights into problems facing the Irish Church today and how those problems ought to be addressed and overcome.

It is true to say that pastorals of the bishops in the recent past have focused realistically on the present situation encountered by the contemporary Irish Church – the situation of the emergence of a 'New Roman Catholicism'. That situation involves '... a culture which pressurises people to push their religious convictions to the private side of their lives'[50] to produce 'a country that is Catholic but not Christian'.[51] Indeed, the dichotomy between the faith that is professed and the faith that is lived in Ireland is, today, a source of serious concern for the Irish bishops. This is especially true in the areas of social justice and sexual morality.

The fact that there is a growing fall-off in the numbers regularly receiving the sacraments is also a source of deep anxiety. This is expressed well by the Archbishop of Dublin who, in a recent Christmas message, devoted his energies to asking lapsed Catholics to return to formal Church structures and sacraments – 'come home to stay'.[52]

Thus, the problems facing Irish Catholicism are well known to the hierarchy – they do not have to rely on sociological surveys to point out the weaknesses of the system. The actual strategies adapted by the bishops to overcome what many writers call 'the crisis of faith' are of significant interest to this study.

Bishops acknowledge the fact that the theology, vision and insights of Vatican II are 'far from being fully or even adequately understood' by laity and clergy alike and, as such, is a major obstacle opposing the current task of Christian renewal.[53] Thus, the necessity of introducing the richness of the vision of Vatican II into every aspect of Irish life has become a priority. The process of initiating and maintaining such renewal is, fundamentally, an educational endeavour and has been recognised as such by the hierarchy.

With this in mind the old reliance on the school system to single-handedly form Christians has come under close scrutiny from Irish bishops:

> ... formation can no longer be left solely to our schools as many parents have left it in the past ... To make religious education effective in our schools nothing less than a co-ordinated and structured undertaking between parents, schools and the parishes which the schools serve can achieve this aim.[54]

Not only does the parish, school and parents share the responsibilities of forming Christians but the community, itself, plays a vital role:

> In every form of education, it is ultimately the community which educates and if the community does not fulfil its proper role the whole process of education is weakened.[55]

Acknowledging this communal role in education is fully in line with Vatican II's model of Christian education as Christian initiation which takes place in the midst of a faith community.

The need to educate the community at large, i.e. children and adults alike, is well known. Vatican II's priority to adult catechesis as the 'chief form of catechesis – because it is addressed to persons who have the greatest responsibilities and and capacity to live the Christian message to its most fully developed form'[56] – is acknowledged.

As early as September 1980, shortly after his installation as bishop of Cork and Ross, Bishop Murphy identified catechetics in general and adult religious education in particular as one priority area of pastoral activity.[57] In 1982, the Bishop of Elphin was able to summarise: 'The greatest pastoral need at present, in this diocese, as indeed in all Ireland, is adult Catholic education.' He outlined the pastoral and liturgical events in the diocese which he saw as presenting an opportunity for such catechesis.[58] In the same year the Bishop of Kerry outlined a three-year adult religious formation programme for use in his diocese. The aim of this programme was to help lay people become more aware of their role and responsibilities within the Church.[59]

In 1983 the diocese of Armagh set up an adult religious education commission. This commission offered a two-year training course at four centres in the diocese. The objectives of the course were:[60]

(a) To prepare members of the laity and clergy who would form a part of a parish team to facilitate the emergence of an informed dynamic local church.

(b) To facilitate the personal Christian formation of the participants.

(c) To enable participants examine the relevance of the Christian message to the life of the local community today.

(d) To facilitate the development of local adult religious educators or leaders in the ministry of education.

The subject of adult catechesis was judged to be of sufficient importance to merit it becoming the basis of a Pastoral Letter from the Bishop of Kerry in 1986. Likewise, because of his recognition of 'an urgent need for adult religious education' in his diocese in 1988, the Bishop of Cork appointed a person with full responsibility for adult religious education.[61]

Thus, one witnesses the emergence of a growing awareness, on the part of the Irish hierarchy, of the urgent need for ongoing adult catechesis in Ireland. However, there is no consistent view with regard to what exactly adult catechesis consists of, what its basic aims are or, indeed, what methodologies ought to be employed to suit the Irish context. Certainly there has not been an adequate statement made or strategy offered at Episcopal Conference level. This results (in the case of many bishops) in uncoordinated or (in the case of some bishops) non-existent efforts to catechise adults.

Perhaps 'we are only beginning'[62] but there are still many causes for concern. Most noticeable of all is the fact that, by as recently as 1991, of the 26 dioceses in the country, 11 had yet to discern the need to appoint a person to co-ordinate and oversee the whole area of adult catechesis.[63] Another regrettable fact is the lack of awareness in contemporary episcopal writings and public statements of the urgent necessity of adult catechesis. One would, for example, expect to find some reference to adult catechesis in a work entitled *A Special Concern, The Philosophy of Education: A Christian Perspective* which comes from a bishop who has significant experience in the Irish educational field.[64] However, there is none. Instead, the work (in arguing against non-denominational education) raises more questions about the philosophy of Catholic education than it answers.

In defining one of the chief purposes of education to be to '... communicate and to deepen an appreciation of the nature and dignity of the human person...' it is difficult to understand why 'students' alone and not others are singled out in this connection by Murray as the sole recipients of education. The philosophy of education held by the author is clear: '... adults attempt to prepare young people to live in a world which the adults [themselves] cannot even imagine...'[65] This philosophy of education, to say the least, is not consistent with that proposed by Vatican II or, indeed, by many contemporary secular educationalists.

There is, undoubtedly, a long path to be travelled before the Irish bishops become fully aware of the primacy of, and urgent need for, adult catechesis. Regrettably not every bishop shares the view of the Bishop of Cork who, at the opening of an adult education course in Ballincollig (September, 1988), outlined his understanding of what he was undertaking. He was helping people to embark upon:

... one form of adult religious education. The lectures, as I see it, are only the beginning of a process which will eventually lead to the existence in every parish of a group of trained people who would be there to lead groups of adults in their search for answers. For that is what it is all about, it seems to me, a searching for answers on the part of people who may feel insecure or inadequate in their knowledge of the faith and of how it relates to their lives.[66]

CONCLUSION

One can conclude that the value placed by contemporary Irish society on adult/continuing education was shown, in this chapter, to be very positive. I have drawn attention to the fact that those most likely to engage in such education tended to be female, middle class, middle aged and already highly educated. I have noted that successive governments have acknowledged the value of adult/continuing education and have shown substantial interest in its development.

By and large the development of adult religious education on the other hand has been haphazard and unplanned. The first attempts to provide for it in this country were often made without either state or Church assistance. When adult religious education did emerge it took the form of local communities offering religious studies within the context of other secular subjects. Only later did the Church begin to offer assistance to such endeavours.

In the absence of any planned, coherent strategy in adult religious education emanating from the Irish Episcopal Conference, uncoordinated developments in this area took place at local level in some dioceses. The most successful approaches were those which saw adult religious education as communal and parish-centred. Thus, adult catechesis, inextricably linked to a parish's celebration of its sacraments, emerged as different from, but incorporating, adult religious education.

The methodology which proved most promising in the field of adult catechesis was one which involved an adaptation of Vatican II's post-conciliar *Rite of Christian Initiation of Adults*. Here, in the process of preparing minors for reception of the sacraments of baptism, confirmation and eucharist, the local parish became an initiating community with adults and minors acting as co-educators.

As far as most Irish bishops are concerned the urgent need for adult catechetics is but slowly emerging. There is little evidence to suggest that it has been given primary attention in line with the recommendations of the last Vatican Council. Any assistance given to its development by Irish bishops has largely been in the guise of extra-mural religious studies programmes. Here, evidence suggests that those who attend such courses are those who are least likely to need help with the development of their faith lives.

CHAPTER VI

Keeping the faith:
PAST TRADITIONS, PRESENT SITUATIONS, FUTURE POSSIBILITIES

INTRODUCTION

The Second Vatican Council, in outlining adult catechesis as the chief form of catechesis, introduced a major change in existing catechetical theory and methodology. This change, the implictions of which are just beginning to be felt, is based on a model of Church and a line of theological thought similar to that evident in the early part of the Church's history during the era of the adult catechumenate.

The aim of this final chapter will be to summarise the insights of the council in the area of adult catechesis, to offer recommendations as to how best they may be adopted by the Irish Church within its present-day context and, finally, to answer questions raised earlier in this work but left unresolved.

THE TRIDENTINE LEGACY

The Second Vatican Council [1963-1965], lasting a little over two years, ended an era of Tridentine reform which had been set in place four hundred years previously. The Council of Trent [1545-1563] had a formative and long-lasting influence, the effects of which are still discernable in today's Church. To offer a critique of the sweeping recommendations for change in the field of catechesis introduced by Vatican II, it will be beneficial to review briefly the model of Church already in existence and the catechetical methodology employed at the time that council first convened.

The Council of Trent was the Roman Catholic Church's definitive statement of the Counter Reformation. Its principal aims were to clarify orthodox teaching, to reaffirm the (Roman) Catholic identity and to consolidate the unity of the Church in the wake of the fragmentation precipitated by the Protestant Reformation. Trent was eager not merely to state Catholic doctrine, but to mould the hearts and minds of the faithful according to a definite model of Church. The model had the Catholic Church referred to in terms such as 'the true Spouse of Christ our Lord, our Holy Mother, the Hierarchical Church'. Such terminology is paralleled in the 'Rules for thinking within the Church' – a chapter appended to the *Spiritual Exercises* of St Ignatius Loyola. These 'Rules' in the opinion of one commentator, Tynan,[1] best sum up the spirit of 'Tridentine things'.

The faithful were encouraged by the 'Rules' to forego all personal judgement and to obey the Church in all things. Not only were they encouraged to accept Church teaching uncritically, but they were also expected to defend actively and uncritically those same teachings:

> We must praise all the commandments of the Church, and be on the alert to find reasons to defend them, and by no means to criticise them.[2]

However, the 'Rules' did recognise the value of modern research. They did acknowledge the work of scholastic doctors and the advantage they enjoyed in interpreting the 'sources of Holy Scripture, the teachings of the saints and the decisions, definitions and decrees of the Church'.[3]

Paradoxically, in Ireland, the opportunity to continue this 'modern research' by the study of theology, was confined to clergy and religious by the 1908 Universities Act.[4] This act prohibited the colleges of the National University from establishing departments of theology. This left the Pontifical University at St Patrick's College, Maynooth, Trinity College, Dublin and Queen's University, Belfast as the only universities providing courses in theology. Since Maynooth College, for the greater part of its history, was closed to the laity and Catholics were discouraged by their bishops from attending Trinity College, there was effectively no opportunity for lay people to study theology in Ireland until comparatively recently. This happened in the case of Maynooth in the late sixties when it opened its theology faculty to lay people. But even then, religious and laity did not and still do not share the same lectures or study for the same qualifications.[5] In the case of Trinity College, from the late sixties, Archbishop McQuaid's prohibition was relaxed and Catholics attended the University in larger numbers and occasionally read theology. In 1981 the College established a non-denominational department of theology with a Roman Catholic as head.

The admission of lay people to theological faculties and departments represented a major step forward, since the Council of Trent discouraged the lay faithful from entering theological debate. The advice of Trent for the laity on this matter was summarised by the 'Rules' in the principle: to achieve truth in all things provided that 'What seems to be white I will believe black if the Hierarchical Church so defines it'.[6]

The legacy of Trent was a strong and united Church. The authority of the clergy and the obedient dependence of the laity were clearly delineated and deeply rooted. The large numbers of priests and religious, especially in the field of education, ensured that the laity were not crucial to the work of catechesis.

Thus, Catholic catechesis since Trent had functioned almost exclusively as if faith were synonymous with belief – belief understood as cognitive assent to doctrinal statements. In the words of Trent's Catechism, faith is an 'unhesitating assent to whatever the authority of our Holy Mother, the Church, teaches us to have been revealed by God'.[7]

With faith defined as belief and formulated in authoritative statements, the logical catechetical step was to compile a summary of 'beliefs' in an effort to teach them to people in a rote manner. This is precisely what the Church did for the best part of four hundred years with its catechisms, beginning with the great sixteenth century ones of Trent, Canisius and Bellarmine. That the catechism rendered invaluable service to the Church in certain places and times is undoubtedly true, and that a 'ready at hand' summary of constitutive Catholic beliefs can still be a service is a conviction held by many today. However, it must be remembered that the success of the catechism was largely dependent upon the strong local faith community of the Church which put 'flesh' upon the doctrinal 'bones' of the question and answer text. When such faith communities grew weak the catechism alone could no longer do the task it once did well.

By the end of the Tridentine era the catechetical emphasis lay almost exclusively on the catechism. The approach tended to be abstract and intellectual, focusing on the content of catechesis at the expense of other dimensions. The medium had almost become the message. As the medium became outmoded, the danger was that so too would the message.

VATICAN II: TOWARDS A NEW CATECHESIS

Vatican II, convened by John XXIII in 1963 in a spirit of *aggiornamento* (modernisation), intended readdressing the imbalances which had become entrenched during the Tridentine era. At its broadest, its aim was to make the message and mission of the Church relevant to the modern world, an aim underlined by the title of one of its most important documents, the *Pastoral Constitution of the Church in the Modern World*. The Tridentine emphasis on the divide between clergy and laity was superseded by a renewed emphasis on the notion of the universal priesthood of the baptised.

Even prior to Vatican II, a major shift had occurred in the emphasis placed on the content and method of catechesis. As early as 1936, Jungman had pointed out the weakness of any catechetical approach which sought to deal with one element of catechesis (content or method) to the detriment of the other. Jungmann criticised the then contemporary view which focused almost exclusively on one methodology (the catechism) and also called for a review of the content of catechesis. In his opinion, it was 'Good News' which needed to be communicated rather than abstract truths.[8] He regretted the lack of Christian revelation among Catholic people, a concern echoed later in the writings of Moran, who called for a better theology of revelation to replace a catechetical theory which he saw as advancing by putting 'pious patches on old inadequate definitions of revelation'.[9]

Jungmann's initiative is recognised as the forerunner of what is today known as anthropological catechesis – catechesis which centres on the person and his/her experience. Christ, in his view, is to be sought and found in the reality of life, as well as in the abstractions of doctrine.

The general thrust of catechetics in the post-Vatican II period can be summarised in a single word: process. The word describes a fundamental philosophical and theological view of God and the human person and of the role of catechesis in bringing the human person closer to God. The human person is no longer seen as the insignificant victim of God's wrath and whim, but rather as a cocreator with God, bringing to fulfilment the whole of God's creation. Humanity is now an essential rather than a dispensable part of God's revelation. Process is not just a combination of content and method. It is, rather, a radical view of life itself, which would find its counterpart in schools of psychology such as holism.

The concept of process is implicit in a definition of catechesis which emerged from the documents of Vatican II. *The General Catechetical Directory* defined catechesis as part of the Ministry of the Word. Its function is to develop in the human person a living, explicit and active faith enlightened by doctrine. But catechesis, in turn, is part of a sequential movement beginning with evangelisation and continuing on to liturgy and theology. The movement commences with 'missionary preaching' intended to 'implant the faith for the first time, securing the acceptance of the Word of God'. Catechesis follows, and then liturgy which, in Jungman's definition is, 'the Church's worship expressed in external forms', especially in the eucharistic celebration.[10]

Basic to the Council's renewed approach to catechesis was its understanding of revelation. *The General Catechetical Directory* offered a succinct definition of this concept: Revelation is an 'act whereby God enters into a personal communion with us'.[11] A process view of revelation holds that it is not to be understood on a single level, such as the intellectual. Rather, the experience of revelation must be total, involving the wholeness of one's being; it must be creative, fulfilling and ongoing, even to eternity. A catechesis directed towards this end must be similarly open in its scope. Such an openness is found in the anthropological approach which informed the design of catechetical syllabi and curricula in Ireland in the post Vatican II era as previously outlined.

The new views brought with them their own emphases. From being the concern of a small group within the Church (mainly priests and religious) catechesis now became 'a work for which the whole church must feel responsible and must wish to be responsible'.[12] Focused on Christ, and led by the pope, the responsibility for catechesis was assigned to priests, religious, parents, teachers and the community at large. These catechists were identified and acknowledged in a 1982 Irish Catechetical Syllabus when it named the catechetical agents as the home, the parish and the school.

In Ireland, the actual development of catechetical programmes in recent years can be traced in the changing use of terminology. Before the impact of Vatican II was felt, the titles used to describe religion programmes in schools reflected the content-centred approach. Syllabi featured Religious Knowledge (R.K.), Christian Doctrine (C.D.) and Religious Instruction (R.I.). These gave way to titles which reflected the influence of various pupil-centred approaches and also the broader aims of the new progrmmes. Most schools now feature Religious Education (R.E.) or Catechetics in their timetables. A distinction is usually drawn between these titles and others such as Religious Studies (R.S.) or Divinity (Div.). These distinctions reflect the changing times of increased secularisation and a greater awareness of ecumenism. However, the continued abundance of such titles today point to a grave lack of consensus about the very nature of catechesis/religious education which has been discussed and documented elsewhere.[13]

The confusion about the very nature of catechesis has led to fundamental questions being asked about the right environment for religious education in schools. Is it possible, or even desirable for a Catholic school to provide a Catholic education?, a vital question asked by Gabriel Moran.[14] His conclusion was that the Church's duty is to run good schools rather than 'Catholic' Schools. One cannot but help note that the focus here has been switched from the school as a centre of Catholic education (meaning a place where the 'truths' of the faith are to be found) to the school as a place of Christian witness, which invites the young person to adopt the faith into which she or he has been baptised and which they see exemplified in the lives of their superiors and in the wider school community.

This leads to an inevitable further question about the compatibility of the terms 'religious' and 'education'. Is it possible to justify a confessional religious approach within an acceptable definition of education? It would appear not as true education does not seek to lead to predetermined conclusions but remains always open to dialogue. This is another reason why the word catechesis (a word which encompasses all levels of learning and involves all age groups) is the preferred expression in post-conciliar thought – as opposed to religious education.

VATICAN II'S MODELS OF CHURCH

It would be inaccurate to suggest that Vatican II outlined a single approach to catechesis. In fact, the council debated the topic relatively quickly. Models of catechesis, as ever, are always dependent upon an underlying model of Church. Again, the council did not outline a single model of Church. Rather, the documents it issued reflect different (and, at times, conflicting) ones. Consequently a unique vision of catechesis is understandably difficult to discern. It is desirable, then, that this issue be clarified.

Vatican II did not bring exploration of the mystery of the Church to an end but its documents do provide a good starting point for further exploration. The major problem with the documents of the council is that, in interpreting them, one can too easily approach them in the same manner as the interpretation of the bible was conducted for a great many years in the past. Like the compilation of the bible, it must be remembered that the documents which were the product of the Council appeared at intervals of over three years, that they were the outcome of four separate sessions, that each one represents different degrees of compromise between ever changing views and interests, and that every one of them emerged in a constantly broadening context (broadened at the very least by each preceding document as it appeared).

It is necessary, then, to cease to regard the documents of the Second Vatican Council as if they were a harmonious whole, with chapters from one pen and mind, and paragraphs of equal worth and significance.

In his book *Models of the Church*,[15] Avery Dulles suggests five different models of Church in the light of Vatican II. His conclusion is that while each has its own specific limitations, they all contain some truth. He contends, therefore, that 'by a kind of mental juggling act, we have to keep several models in the air at once'.[16]

It is possible to argue that during the life of the council [October 1962-December 1965] the thinking of the assembly of bishops concerning the nature of the Church, developed in such a way that some of their later views did not simply add to, but actually superseded, some of their earlier ones. This is because not every model of the Church is compatible with every other one.

It is interesting to note that the Constitution on the Sacred Liturgy was the first document of the Council [promulgated on December 4th, 1963]. It would have been very different had it been the last! On reflection, it was an extraordinary enterprise to launch into a renewal of the liturgy without first giving considerable thought to the nature of the Church itself.

It is by no means clear why the Church Fathers decided to approach the topic of the liturgy prior to that of the Church. It is possible that it may be due to the fact that the Preparatory Commission for the Liturgy (created in June 1960) had finished its draft working-document sooner than the Preparatory Commission for Faith and Morals. Thus, its *schema* was one of the seven submitted to the bishops prior to the beginning of the council (in July 1962), whereas the *schema*, *De Ecclesia*, was not distributed until November 23rd, 1962 (five weeks after the council had opened).

Thus, the working model of the Church which underlines the document on the liturgy was one which the Council Fathers themselves would have been brought up with. Presuming that the majority of them had completed their seminary studies prior to World War II they would, then, have shared an acceptance of that model of the Church which dominated Catholic theology until about 1940, as Dulles mentions.[17] Pius XII's encyclical which brought the Mystical Body analogy to the centre was published in 1943. The effects of *Divino Afflante Spiritu*, written in the same year, offered a green light to Catholic scripture scholars to proceed with a biblical interpretation which previously had been regarded with suspicion by Rome. However, the effects of either were not to be felt in seminary education for some years. Apart, then, from the scholarly few, not many of the bishops present at the council could have experienced the force of the biblical way of thinking or talking about the Church.

In 1962, both the Curia and its opponents shared the same model of Church, though they differed about how it should be operated because they had different purposes in mind. The model in question is that of the Church as Institution. In this model, the Church is a society (a perfect society) and, as such, capable of description in terms of analogies drawn from political society. This was the model presupposed in the liturgy debate and the model which is dominant in the Constitution on the Sacred Liturgy, despite the infiltration of different images.

Much of the argument in the course of the council's first session was over the shape of the power structures in the Church seen as a 'perfect society'. Even the pastoral concern of the diocesan bishops (in contrast with the curial bishops) present at the Council did not necessarily indicate a line of thought based on some other model of Church. If pastoral and missionary effort is based on the assumption that there is little or no truth, life or hope outside the boundaries of the Church, the implication is that the Church is perfect-society-centred.

This is explicitly the view of the Church presented in the opening paragraph of the Liturgy Constitution:

> It is the goal of this most sacred Council ... to strengthen those aspects of the Church which can help to summon all of mankind into her embrace.

In the following paragraph, the model of the Church as Sacrament (although that word is not used, only the word 'sign') is cleverly subordinated to the primary model above, and the function of liturgy is defined in that context:

> The liturgy is ... the outstanding means by which the faithful can express in their lives, and manifest to others, the Mystery of Christ and the real nature of the true Church ... To outsiders, the liturgy ... reveals the Church as a sign raised above the nations. Under this sign the scattered sons of God are being gathered into one until there is one fold and one shepherd.

This description does, indeed, represent a modified institutionalism but the underlying assumption of the *sola ecclesia* which runs throughout, cannot escape the accusation of 'triumphalism'.

Today, many theologians feel uncomfortable with that view of the liturgy and the view of the Church which underpins it. It can be argued that, had the fathers debated the liturgy last rather than first (provided they were consistent in developing their later view of Church), they would have produced a very different kind of document. This is possible, because the fathers moved on to embrace a new model of Church, from which point of view everything looks different. The shift took place as as they passed via the Dogmatic Constitution on the Church (which was debated 1-7 December, 1962, 30 September-31 October 1963, and again 15-18 September 1964) to the end of the debate on the Pastoral Constitution on the Church in the Modern World (which occupied two periods of debate, 20 October-10 November 1964 and 22 September-7 October 1965).

When the Dogmatic Constitution on the Church did finally appear in November 1964 it was certainly a remarkable and fruitful modification of the view of the Church as a perfect society, centred on the papal monarchy. Compared with the earlier preoccupation with juridical structures and clerical powers, the Constitution made great advances with the help of images of the Church as the sacrament of union with God and of unity among people, of using biblical language to refer to the Church, of the central position of the People of God (considered prior to any distinction between hierarchy and laity), of setting the papacy in its proper context of the episcopal college, of ministry as a genuine *diakonia* or service, and of elaborating a theology of the laity.

Yet, the ghost of the earlier model is still there. It is qualified, but it is still there. Evidence for this can be found in statements such as the one which opens paragraph 13: 'All men are called to belong to the new People of God'. The long paragraphs 15 and 16 are determined attempts to relate 'all men' to 'the Church' in some degree or other. Or one may consider paragraph 17, which interprets the missionary work of the Church entirely in terms of the objective, 'that the entire world may become the People of God, the Body of the Lord ...' This model is still that in which the Church is the centre and goal of all human history. It suggests that the Church exists to recruit all humankind into its ranks rather than existing to offer service to humankind. Essentially either the Church is the goal or purpose of God's endeavours, or it is a means to God's further purpose; it cannot be both. The final model, therefore, replaces the original one: even if not all the bishops present realised this.

Thus, if the Church is only a means to some further end, and if that end has to do with the union of all humankind in one family (the Family of God) and if the Church's task is to serve humankind with that goal in view – then one can hardly take the view that the Liturgy Constitution took; that 'the liturgy is the summit towards which the activity of the Church is directed' and that 'the goal of apostolic works is that all who are made sons of God by faith and baptism should come together to praise God in the midst of his Church ...'

THE IMPLICIT MODEL OF CHURCH IN
THE RITE OF CHRISTIAN INITIATION OF ADULTS (R.C.I.A.)

Vatican II's final liturgical document (the compilation of which was mandated during the Council[18]) was released on January 6, 1972, the *Rite of Christian Initiation of Adults* (R.C.I.A.). The document contained the restored rites of the ancient adult catechumenate. It is interesting that this final document (which draws, develops and expands upon all previous Council statements) should favour a distinctively new and unambiguous ecclesiology

– and a catechetical methodology based upon it. This ecclesiology is at the same time very ancient and very new – it is as old as the Church, itself, yet had long been forgotten. Of all the Council documents this is probably the most radical, dynamic and challenging. The rite juxtaposes the words *catechesis* and *initiation* and outlines a new model of religious education as initiation into an adult faith community. Undoubtedly, it is towards this document one ought to look today for a workable model of catechesis – particularly within the Irish context. The vibrant ecclesiology of the Rite will now be recalled.

The Rite, promulgated by Paul VI, offers a vigorous vision of the Christian community and a realistic image of the Christian faith. With the publication of the document, the 'requested revisions' of Vatican II were completed. In the case of this rite it was a matter of keeping the best wine until last. The documents of Vatican II created a vision for the twentieth century Church. Ten years on, reform completed and renewal beginning, the final liturgical document emerging from the Council gives shape and form to that vision.

The *Rite of Christian Initiation of Adults* offers a new (or perhaps, more accurately, renewed) ecclesiology. An integral part of this ecclesiology is a reversal to an earlier practice of Christian initiation with the catechetical emphasis being placed upon adults. The actual (sacramental) celebration of initiation comes at the completion, rather than at the inception of a process and celebrates the conversion to Christian life. There is no medieval presupposition that being born into a Christian family guarantees the future choice of living as a Christian. No longer is physical presence the only requirement for the valid reception of the sacraments of initiation.

Reading between the lines, one detects a grave concern to guard against the indiscriminate administration of the sacraments of which the Church is steward and custodian. There appears to be an admission that there is no birthright to membership in the Church, but that membership is a privilege to be worked for and won by a fundamental conversion, a commitment, and actions commensurate with the gospel.

One can not remain blind to the radical change in first principles contained in the new Rite, changes on both the practical and theoretical levels. Conversion precedes and continues beyond preparation for, and celebration of, initiation; only upon successful instruction and a consequent concrete decision to live as a Christian are the sacraments received. As a guide, the Rite proposes a three year period for initiation. The energy of endurance and conditioning emerging from prayer and action will nourish the candidates for the difficult task of living as Christians for the whole of their lives in a contemporary world which so often opposes Christian values.

The Church of the second to sixth centuries knew well the responsibilities of preparing individual adults to live as Christians in a pagan world. One should not think it strange that the new Rite bears many resemblances to the process employed in this era and draws heavily from its model and rich tradition. Being a Christian will no longer mean being baptised, being confirmed and receiving the eucharist. It will also mean (according to this Rite) being converted, sealed in the Spirit and becoming seriously committed to living as a Christian.

The second major asset of the Rite vis-a-vis ecclesiology, and one closely allied to its vision of initiation as a process, lies in the manifold variety of individuals involved in the process. The Rite calls for an actualisation and acceptance of pluriform ministries and gifts in the local Church.

Contemporary initiation tends to be an individualistic and private affair extending itself only to the priest, parents and godparents. The 1972 Rite repeatedly and vigorously stresses the responsibility of the whole community in the whole initiation process. Paragraph 4 states that initiation takes place 'within the community of the faithful' who are, themselves, intimately involved and serve as examples for the catechumens.

The point is clear and has already been stressed. However, one should note the language used in the document. Firstly, it uses the term 'People of God' and correlates this to the 'local Church'. Secondly, this local Church should 'always understand and demonstrate that the initiation of adults is the concern of all the baptised'. Thirdly, this concern is identified with the Church's apostolic mission, i.e., making Christians. Finally, this vocation is given not only to the Church as a whole, but to each disciple of Christ.

Beyond the general involvement of the whole community in the initiation process, the Rite singles out various individuals who bear a great responsibility in the formation of new Christians: sponsor, godparent, bishop, presbyter, deacon and catechist. Each individual performs a personal ministry rather than a function in the initiation process. Paragraph 42 requires 'If the sponsor is not to fulfill his or her ministry for the remainder of the catechumenate, another person takes on this responsibility'. It is important to note that the Rite presents the ministry of the godparent as a public office requiring testimony before the community. This responsibility continues after baptism, and is associated with the call to fidelity. The godparent's role is placed beyond mere friendship into an official public environment.

If, as already outlined, initiation is considered as a process, the ministerial functions in this process are considered as varied, encompassing, and collegial. In short, the ecclesial image of ministry in the initiation process is participatory. The document calls for the activation of a spectrum of possible ministries in the Church. The rite presents a grass roots ecclesiology, emphasising the communal structure of the Church and recognising the variety of gifts in the local Church. This is an ecclesiology of involvement and witness, an ecclesiology which invites and elicits participation from below and within, rather than from without and above. This is an ecclesiology where theory is wedded with practice; a community and Church based on both sociability and comradeship. This is a Church which, itself, continues its baptism and conversion through its ministry to those who wish to be within its membership, a Church which continually confronted with making new Christians will, itself, be called to hearken back to its origins.

Where the Decree on Ministries in the Church created a potential, the 1972 Rite actualises this vision in reality and in a manner which places ministry at the heart of the local Church. One further ecclesiological point merits consideration. The Rite presents the local Church as a liturgical-sacramental Church. This appears in a variety of ways. Foremost, the local community is involved in a ritual in the fullest meaning of the word. The Church is performing its work, which is making Christians. The Church is being itself, i.e., the community which, having been called to God, now extends that call through its proclamation and explanation of the gospel in concrete situations to all peoples. It does this not as individuals, as such, but as a community.

The liturgical-sacramental orientation of the Rite will, of course, effect ecclesiology. Since initiation takes place in the midst of that community, it is embellished by the liturgical life of the community. The Rite allows the liturgy to return to, and be an expression of, the concrete life of the community. Above all other liturgical seasons, Lent and Easter experience a revival of meaning and depth. The Rite links real life and liturgical/sacramental action as the Church fulfils its practical mission of preaching the gospel and adding to its members through the sacraments of initiation.

Realistically, the threat posed to the implementation of the Rite is threefold. Firstly, some will look upon the document as just another 'rubrical change' issued from Rome and fail to understand ecclesial implications of the decree. Secondly, the Rite changes in a fundamental manner the present understanding of what catechesis is all about. In fact, it changes the first principles. Thirdly, some will notionally assent to the theological orientation of the document but reject it on pragmatic grounds, pointing to the massive educational task demanded if the document is ever to even begin to be implemented. The threats are both clear and real: lack of understanding, fear and pragmatism.

SACRAMENTS, SACRAMENTALITY, INITIATION AND FORMATION

Four major insights relating to the understanding and practice of Christian initiation, deriving from the introduction of the R.C.I.A. into Catholic life, can be summarised as follows: the reunification of the sacraments of baptism, confirmation and eucharist; the establishment of a concrete relationship between ritual event and initiatory process; the recovery of the communal dimension of Christian life and the preference given to Christian formation over doctrinal instruction. In short, the document outlines a concrete educative relationship that exists between Christian life and the administration of the sacraments – and not just the sacraments of initiation.

Paragraph 19 of the *Rite of Christian Initiation of Adults*, quoting the Decree on Missions, *Ad Gentes*, of the Council (par. 13) refers primarily to the time of the catechumenate and states that it ought to bring about a 'transition that brings with it progressive changes in outlook and style of life which should become evident by a gradual evolution over a period of time'. The principle stated applies to the whole process of initiation as well as to the rest of ecclesial life.

Here one witnesses something of the sense of dynamism restored to sacramental theology. The implication is that no single sacrament, by itself, discloses its root-meaning in isolation from those that precede and succeed it within the ongoing communal spiritual journey of conversion that is ecclesial life.

If one considers the underlining ecclesiology and sacramentality implicit in the post-conciliar rite, it is possible to argue that the entire life of a follower of Christ is an ongoing process of initiation which begins at the moment of birth and ends at the moment of death. Thus, one is continually in a process of *becoming* a Christian. The sacraments, then, are rites which mark the end of one and the beginning of another stage of ongoing initiation. *All* sacraments are communal in nature and can only be celebrated within a communal context. This understanding can accommodate confirmation being conferred *after* the reception of the eucharist, although perhaps, within this context, it might be more fruitful to confer it later in adulthood.

Other sacraments like marriage can also be understood to represent a further step in Christian Initiation. In this case, initiation into a union that symbolises the relationship between Christ and his Church. Penance is an example of a sacrament which is received many times in life. On each occasion a further and deeper commitment to Christian living is made. The sacrament of the sick which, in the light of Vatican II, can be conferred on any person who is in danger (not necessarily from death) (*cf.* Canon 998 of the 1983 *Code of Canon Law*) also marks a further stage in Christian formation – initiation into sickness, pain and suffering which is so central to the heart of Christianity.

Likewise, it is possible to understand the sacrament of Holy Orders as a further sacrament of initiation into Christian living. Some commentators have suggested that the catechumenate of the early Church never actually died but rather found its way into seminaries and houses of religious formation.[19] Many contemporary views on priestly formation are based upon a rediscovery of that fact. As early as 1977, Charles Bouchard looked favourably on the model of religious formation as an extension of the *Rite of Christian Initiation of Adults*.[20] What Bouchard suggested was that seminary and novitiate formation be approached in the same manner as initiation into the Church. In other words, ongoing Christian formation for service in priestly ministry is to be achieved in stages which parallel the stages of initiation outlined in the R.C.I.A.

More recently, in the Irish context, the same analogy has been made. Eugene Duffy draws attention to the need for the process of priestly formation to change in order to meet the vastly different circumstances of today's world. Like Bouchard, he juxtaposes the four stages of the new rite of adult initiation with suggested stages of priestly formation.[21]

Perhaps the most serious (and disturbing) examination of the whole question of religious formation has been conducted by Donal Dorr. Dorr's view is that 'at present, in much of the Western world, the Church has formation programmes without people to make use of them and people without programmes available to them'.[22] Here he suggests that the present formation programmes in seminaries have difficulty finding candidates to fill them while lay people, who clearly also desire continuous formation, are devoid of any such possibilities.

For Dorr, it is a matter of justice that the question of how the formation resources of the Christian community are being used be examined. He claims that the Church's resources of expertise, time, energy, buildings and finance ought to be evenly divided between the three main groups of Christian people who are in need of formation, i.e. clerics, religious and laity. He believes the latter are, at present, being 'neglected' because

> ... the kind of formation that is widely offered to lay leaders ... often consists of a series of evening lectures once or twice a week over a period of months. It is neither fair nor realistic to expect people to feel qualified and competent to engage in various lay ministries after such meagre courses. Training for ministry has to be taken more seriously than that.[23]

However, nobody could reasonably expect lay leaders to go through the kind of specialised formation programmes that are at present required for clergy or for members of religious communities. Such programmes are organised according to a pattern that makes them more or less inaccessible to the majority of lay Christians. It is important, then, that suitable formation programmes be designed which will be of real benefit to local communities and will include, where possible, lay leaders, clergy, seminarians and members of religious congregations. This is fully consistent with the vision of Christian formation in the R.C.I.A. which posits formation in the midst of the community – not removed from it. Clearly what is in question here is co-formation.

THE PARISH AND SACRAMENTS OF ADULTHOOD

In the past, the parish has focussed almost all of its educational efforts, and a significant amount of its sacramental ministry, on childhood. Naturally, then, it may feel helpless in the face of a contemporary demand for adult catechesis which is implicit in the 1972 *Rite of Christian Initiation of Adults*. A re-understanding of the meaning of sacraments and of sacramental ministry may re-order an educational future for the parish as a viable believing community of adults into which minors are to be sacramentally initiated. The underlining assumption in the 1972 rite is that the Church is primarily an adult community, celebrating adult sacraments. The task of the Church is, by means of its sacraments, to continue the faith development of those present as well as to initiate new members into that faith community.

In the light of Vatican II's *Rite of Christian Initiation of Adults* it is possible to parallel sacraments to rites of passages.[24] Sacraments, in different religious traditions, have historically arisen as the attempts of a community to help people through the dangerous passages encountered in their lives. The sacraments of baptism and confirmation, for example, in the Christian tradition focus on the crucial passages into life and community and into puberty and adulthood. The community recognises these as crucial moments (as are those into marriage, priesthood and death) and wishes to help the individual through the passage.

Several points are of interest in such an interpretation. Firstly, it seems that it is the community which sees the person through the crucial passage. The community elects a representative to *perform* the rite, itself, but the person is empowered *through* the passage *by* the community.

At stake here (at least within Christianity) is the question of who performs the rite or sacrament. To say that the priest performs the rite is only partially true (*cf* the Rite of Marriage where the partners administer the sacrament). In a very real sense (though, regrettably, as yet little explored) the community performs the sacrament.[25] Thus, a priest cannot baptise a child who will not enjoy a Christian community whose sign and witness makes the baptism effective. Likewise, the youth who is confirmed in a community which gives little Christian witness is not effectively confirmed. This analysis is not meant to denigrate the importance of the priest in the rite, but rather to relieve him of an improper onus. He cannot do what is for the community to do, namely, to effect the sacrament. Historically, Roman Catholics have come to understand the sacramental ministry of the Church in an increasingly individualistic fashion – as the ministry of the priest only, apart from the efficacious and essential engagement of the power of the community.

Another example of what is being suggested relates to the eucharist. The priest alone can not bring about what he signifies in that celebration. Only the community can effect and celebrate this brotherhood. Thus, it is the sacramental power of the community at large that one must explore when the parish as sacrament is considered.

Implicit in such an understanding of sacrament (one which shifts some of the responsibility for the rite from the priest to the community) is, again, the vision of a sacrament as not merely performed in one moment of time but rather over a long process. As the priest (as celebrant) is most formally related to the ritual moment, so the community (as continuous sign) is most formally related to the process aspect of the sacrament. It remains to theology to explore this relation of rite and process vis-a-vis Christian sacraments.

In a real sense, then, a person is baptised into a Christian community only gradually. This suggests that it takes time to become a Christian. Likewise, confirmation as a further initiation into the powerfulness of Christian adulthood is a gradual process. Only gradually does the adolescent make the transition from childhood to the dangerously powerful stage of young adulthood. The sacrament as effective sign occurs in this process. The rite of confirmation attempts to focus on this transition and in doing so hopes to empower the individual to navigate it successfully.

The passage is, of course, successfully navigated over a number of years and then only if a caring community leads the way. It is this 'leading the way' as sign and witness that the sacramental function of the Christian community needs to be further investigated.

One possible way of conceiving the relationship of priest and community in the execution of the sacraments is as follows. The priest, as representative of the people, in his performance of the rite, initiates the sacrament.[26] In the years surrounding this rite of celebration, the community effects the sacrament. The notion of the effectiveness of the community in the performance of sacraments requires much more elaboration than can be provided here. For the moment, one must be content with indicating the central importance of the community in effecting sacraments – a theme that has received too little attention in the past.

Such an understanding of sacraments, then, has adults as the chief recipients and, to a less extent, minors who are being initiated into an adult Church. The sacraments, themselves, are effected by the wider community at large.

R.C.I.A. AS MODEL OF SACRAMENTAL INITIATION OF MINORS

It is clear that the *Rite of Christian Initiation of Adults* is a rite that gives shape, articulation and fundamental meaning to all the other ones which constitute the Roman initiatory economy. If this is true, then it represents a crucial restoration in the way Roman Catholics think about sacramental reality. Rather than regarding sacraments as separate entities, each containing its own exclusive meaning for theological exploitation (as in the case of the Rite of Confirmation), the *Rite of Christian Initiation of Adults* presumes that all the initiatory rites form one closely articulated whole which, in turn, relates intimately with all the other non-initiatory sacraments and rites. Not only does this mean that infant baptism must be seen anew (perhaps as a legitimate abnormality out of which too many conclusions should not be drawn in theory or in practice) but that confirmation as well must be re-evaluated in a more rigorously baptismal context – the same context from which it gradually became separated in the West prior to the Scholastic period.

The Rite, in paragraph 34, speaks of the inextricable connection between the sacraments of baptism and confirmation:

> By this connection is signified the unity of the Paschal Mystery, the necessity that obtains between the mission of the Son and the pouring out of the Holy Spirit, and the joint relationship of the sacraments [of baptism and confirmation] by each divine Person comes with the Father upon the baptised.

If the theology expressed here is to be taken seriously for what it says, then it is inevitable that the continued separation of baptism in infancy from confirmation in youth deserves to be reviewed. The alternative will be to sustain, at the same time, two quite different sets of meanings, catecheses and ritual forms for the sacrament of confirmation. The first will be that for adults, who are baptised and confirmed within the same service even if the bishop is absent: the ethos of this ritual form of confirmation is very obviously baptismal, paschal and trinitarian. The second will be that for children and adolescents who were already baptised several years previously: the ethos of this ritual form of confirmation has more to do with its marking an educational or life-crisis point in the development of the recipients by an episcopal presidency at the event.

In other words, the Roman Church now finds itself affirming in practice two initiatory theories and practices that have successively held sway in its history: the first is antique and paschal, the second medieval and socio-personal in practice. The first presupposes the presence of adult converts in local churches, the second presupposes a sustained Catholic birthrate and functioning forms of religious education such as the local parish and the Catholic school.

The implications of such contrasts go far beyond sacramental practice in the narrow sense. Both sets of initiatory theories and practices now embraced by the Roman Church rest upon rather different views of the Church and its situation in the world. If, as in the medieval period in the West, the Church could reasonably presume to be correlative with the society of which it was largely the author, then it could and did expect that evangelisation and catechesis would be conducted on many levels throughout a society based on Christian assumptions. The Church itself, in such a situation, could direct its attention toward keeping the *foci* of social-political power reasonably Christian in order that preaching and exhortation to more devout piety within the Chuch might function freely. The medieval policy was, to put it another way, directed not so much at strategic conversion to the faith as at tactical conversions within the faith to lives of greater piety and more intense devotion, as exhibited in the abundance of religious orders and pious lay movements of the day.

In a real sense, the ancient baptismal catechumenate never died: rather it was adopted and adapted by houses of religious formation, becoming the novitiate and later, a seminary education.[27] By the same token, religious vows and priestly ordination took on much of the aura once possessed by baptism – a development (legitimate or otherwise) that has returned to the centre stage of theological debate in the demand of women for priestly ordination, a demand often based on a perceived understanding of baptism creating a Christian proletariat while holy orders creates something often viewed as 'first-class citizenship' in the Church. In this, one detects a medieval sacramental theology taken to not illogical extremes. However, the more antique set of initiatory theories and practices dating back to a period prior to the emergence of a medieval 'Christiandom' (when the correlation of Church and civil society either did not exist or was only just beginning) in no way posits such clear divisions. The baptismal writings surviving from this period (especially those of Tertullian, Cyril of Jerusalem, Chrysostom, Ambrose and Augustine) attest presumptions that held evangelisation and catechesis (both aspects of sacramental ministry) to be the task of the entire local Church.

Within the Irish context, the idea of sacramental initiation of minors into the Church, based on the educational insights of the R.C.I.A., holds many possibilities. But these possibilities may, of necessity, indicate that the days of baptism in infancy and confirmation in adolescence as a norm are numbered; that the days of catechising solely in school classrooms are numbered; that the days in which one regards a man's or woman's entry into novitiate or seminary as their 'entry into the Church' are numbered.

R.C.I.A. AS MODEL OF ADULT CHRISTIAN FORMATION

It has already been suggested that the R.C.I.A. may serve as a model to initiate minors into a vibrant and living Church. For adults who are already sacramentally initiated, the same rite can serve as a model of how the process of Christian formation may continue throughout life's journey.

Basic to the approach of the R.C.I.A. is the theme of communal spiritual journey. The rite of initiation is suited to the spiritual journey of adults (even adults who are already sacramentally initiated) – a journey which varies according to the many forms of God's grace, the free co-operation of the individual, the action of the Church and the circumstances of time and place. The four periods outlined in the R.C.I.A. offer the environment not only for the growth and conversion of those journeying into the Christian community but also a model for continued growth and conversion of the entire members of that community.

The four periods of the R.C.I.A., already examined, should not be viewed in a mere chronological order. Conversion, for example, may happen many times and in many ways, not just after making initial enquiry about the Christian faith. Rather, such periods are dimensions of a process into and out of which people move with their own freedom and the summons of the Holy Spirit.

The spiritual journey of all Christians is marked by steps/occasions/sacraments which stand out and may act as opportunities of growth. Ideally, in the light of the R.C.I.A., such growth is facilitated by the presence and activity of a strong local Christian community (within the Irish context this proves problematical). At the time of marriage, for example, the parish should be able to offer the couple preparing for the sacrament other couples who would meet with them to share their faith and to discuss the impact their faith has on their love, on the way they communicate and on their children. Similarly at the time of death, the parish should be able to offer the widow or widower other people who have lost a spouse and who will share their faith and who will outline what impact their faith has on their loneliness, on their loss and on their need to keep on living and growing.

Ideally a living parish ought to have neighbourhood communities who meet regularly to share their faith and to establish how that faith can lead to concrete service in their neighbourhood. Apparently, the most exciting movements in the Catholic Church today involve those kinds of small communities which offer a personal experience of faith: Marriage Encounter, Charismatic groups, Search Retreats, Bible Study Groups, prayer groups and so on. These function often alongside or, indeed, outside parish structures. This was also shown to be the case in Ireland.

Faith itself is, in a very real way, the acceptance of God's presence in one's personal journey through life. Faith accepts that one's unique life journey and life experiences are part of the greater web of God's journey. Faith is a personal surrender to the fact that one does not entirely control one's life journey. Parishes, catechumenates, the best programmes in catechesis do not, by themselves, produce faith. They can offer the environment where one can explore one's unique life journey, question its meaning, listen to the biographies of others, including Jesus', to see if they cast light on one's personal journey. However, the response of faith is totally one's own. It is a conversion, a turning toward God as the source of the past, the author of the present and the ground of future experiences. Faith is also more than intelligence, more than 'acceptance of truths on the authority of God revealing' as both Trent and Vatican I saw it.

Rather, faith is encountered by a continuous on-going conversion and formation. Conversion itself is a process. There is no one-time conversion. Holding a dead child, losing a job, entering a marriage, watching children grow up and leave home, accepting a religious vocation or commitment, beginning a new life at retirement, parting company with a life-long companion are all moments in a life-long process of conversion and formation. Again and again one is summoned to ponder one's story, struggle with its inherent questions, listen to the experiences of the journeys of others and make a surrender of faith that there is, indeed, Good News – Good News that life is more powerful than death and that God gives everlasting life. This is why the R.C.I.A. is clearly a model for all adult growth because it speaks the same language and holds the same model of Christian formation as a life-long communal journey of conversion. Vibrant local Christian communities and parishes are the principal *loci* for such growth and conversion.

ADULT FAITH: THE IRISH CONTEXT

The urgent need for co-ordinated adult catechesis at local level in the contemporary Church should, at this stage, be evident. As far as Ireland is concerned that need is but slowly emerging. Sociological surveys relating to faith and practice have continued to indicate an ever weakening sense of Christian identity, a growing sense of secularism and an overall decline in sacramental participation – in short, Christian faith in modern Ireland is beginning to weaken and lose possession of the strong roots from which it once proudly grew and flourished. Instead a 'new generation of Catholics' is emerging who look less and less to their Church for guidance in everyday matters. The result is that the gap between the faith that is handed down and the faith that is lived continues to widen as time progresses towards the end of this century. The need to re-evaluate the present catechetical system in order to cope with new situations and new demands is evidently urgent.

It is now some thirty years since the opening of Vatican II by Pope John XXIII. In the sphere of religion little has changed in Ireland during that time. True, the altars have been turned around and the Mass is now said in English (and Irish). For the average person this is the sum-total of the Council's reforms. Much of the insights and richness of Vatican II have either been misunderstood or not yet taken as seriously as they deserve – this has been shown to be particularly true in the area of catechesis. It is interesting to witness most criticism relating to the failure at implementing the insights of Vatican II coming from lay theologians who appear to be very aware of, and concerned about, the weaknesses of today's Irish Church.[28]

The problem is not quite so simplistic as discerning and implementing the recommendations of Vatican II. It has been shown that the documents of the council reveal more than one model of Church giving rise to more than one catechetical model. The model of Church preferred in this work is that implicit in the final liturgical document to emerge from Vatican II, the *Rite of Christian Initiation of Adults*.

The situation is further complicated because it appears that Rome itself has done a U-turn on many of the insights and recommendations advanced by the council. A crucial one documented in this work is the recent attempt to return to the catechism approach to Christian education, and more regrettably still a universal catechism approach!

CONTINUED DEPENDENCE ON THE CATHOLIC SCHOOLING SYSTEM

The Irish Church, by and large, has continued to utilise an educational methodology based on the model of Christian education put in place by the Council of Trent. The model is that of Christian education as instruction in doctrines of faith. The associated methodology finds its *locus* within the primary and secondary Catholic school systems. Although such an approach worked (and, undoubtedly, worked well) in the past that does not give it a right to be unquestioningly implemented today when the contemporary context has changed so rapidly. What can be easily forgotten is that the Catholic schooling system in the past was supported by a deeply faith-committed society. Today the existence of such can no longer be taken for granted. Therefore, major efforts at making an old system work in new circumstances may not succeed. I have argued that the catechetical needs of the adult community must first be addressed as a matter of priority, as Vatican II recommended. This offers the possibility of the development and formation of a strong adult faith community worthy of initiating minors into and perhaps, more importantly, a community which minors desire to be part of.

In Ireland resources (financial and otherwise) are still being utilised to prop up what many consider to be an outdated and lame model of Christian education. Instead of catechesis being parish-centred it still remains almost exclusively school-centred. Thus, one continues to witness school 'religion classes' being conducted outside of, and removed from, a parish faith community. Boarding schools continue to remove children from faith communities to give them a 'Christian education' in artificial surroundings. Large numbers of clergy and religious continue to be deployed in schooling systems which are no longer capable of doing what they once did well – for the reasons already outlined.

Perhaps the best (and saddest) indicator of the effort to re-enforce the Catholic school system is the attempt to introduce Religious Studies as an exam subject in an attempt to solve the 'crisis in religious education'. Such a move would confirm the image of catechesis as academic and examinable – in this case examinable not by a faith community but by the State! This understanding of catechesis already exists in the minds of many 'catechists' whose qualifications are the possession of a primary degree in theology and a higher diploma in education (designed as it is to facilitate the 'teaching' of secular subjects). The equation of Theology + Education = Catechesis is a false one. Catechesis requires, but is greater than, both theology and education. Aware of this fact, institutions like Mater Dei today offer catechetical courses which encompass both spheres fully.

In short, the role played by the Catholic schooling system deserves to be reviewed and placed within a larger context of parish catechesis, i.e. the role played by the Catholic school is only part of a broader formation process which the local parish community is ultimately responsible for.

KEEPING THE FAITH: THE WAY FORWARD

Christian faith in Ireland, if it is to be again as strong as it once was, may have to be seen less as a set of doctrines to be learned and more as a discipleship to be lived and learned in the midst of a worshipping community. In fact, 'live and learn' might be an apt phrase to capture the approach of the R.C.I.A. – a document from which the Irish Church can benefit greatly by its adaptation and implementation. The key paragraph of the R.C.I.A. is number nineteen of the *General Introduction* which, in four segments, outlines an holistic programme of formation. This programme includes doctrinal and moral instruction integrated with reflection on experience, initiation into prayer (both public and private), the discovery of gospel values, and much more. Not only is this formation multi-dimensional, it is also circular rather than linear; its objectives are best met not by a graduated programme of instruction but by a series of explorations that radiate outwards from the gospels into every area of personal, ecclesial and social living.

Thus, the model of Christian education favoured by Vatican II, that of education as on-going formation for adults and eduction as initiation for minors, deserves to be taken seriously within the Irish context. Adult catechesis as the 'chief form of catechesis ... towards which all other catechesis is directed' ought not be let remain words on a page but merit the opportunity to be given life and reality. Such a catechesis, it is envisaged, will be accommodated to the communal liturgical celebration of the community's sacraments.

Undoubtedly, a promising way forward in the field of adult catechesis in this country lies in adapting the R.C.I.A. to particular local situations. It should not be forgotten that one of the most frequently used words in the Rite is 'adapt'. It has been noted that the Rite has already been very successfully adapted in some Irish dioceses (e.g. Dublin and Ossory). The greatest challenge, then, is to adapt it to local circumstances in order to initiate minors and continue to help in the Christian formation of adults who are already sacramentalised but who may not yet be catechised.

The attention given to adult catechesis in this country in the past has been both limited and narrow and in sharp contrast to that proposed in the R.C.I.A. It has consisted mainly of the provision of extra-mural programmes of religious studies. Here, it was noted that the people who generally attended were those least in need of help with the ongoing process of developing their faith. Other approaches which proved more successful in attracting a wider sociological distribution of adults were those which sought to actively involve parents in the sacramental preparation of their children.

Realistically, the futuristic enactment of the R.C.I.A. may not be rapid or facile. Enormous energy, dedication, time and experimentation will be required. But the approach merits serious consideration and a beginning ought to be made somewhere. The theology of the document is sound. The model of the Church outlined is vibrant, alive and participatory. The effectiveness of the document lies in the court of the future. All forces in the Irish Church including bishops, theologians, educators and pastors, ought to realise the task at hand and begin the necessary work. The *Rite of Christian Initiation of Adults* challenges us to look not at 'something' but rather at ourselves, the Church upon which we stand, the Church which we are.

Thus, if the Spirit of Vatican II in relation to catechesis is to be given flesh in Ireland then the following recommendations merit serious consideration:

1. The appointment of adult catechists in all Irish dioceses to develop and co-ordinate the entire field of adult catechesis. This work has suggested that adult catechesis be modelled on the final liturgical document to emerge from Vatican II, the 1972 *Rite of Christian Initiation of Adults*.

2. Such catechists should be competent in the inter-related disciplines of theology, education and catechesis.

3. The functions of the diocesan adult catechist ought to include:

(a) To educate Christians (both clergy and laity) about the urgency of, and basis for, adult catechesis.

(b) To assist parishes in developing adult catechetical programmes best suited to their needs – the adaptation of the R.C.I.A. appears to offer the most potential. The primary aim of such programmes would be to assist ongoing Christian formation of adults and Christian initiation of minors.

(c) To co-ordinate primary and secondary school catechesis and help centre such catechesis in the local parish. Most dioceses already have clergy, religious or lay people in charge of primary and secondary school catechesis. The task of the adult catechist would be to work with such people through existing channels in order to secure the objectives mentioned above.

(d) To co-ordinate and utilise the catechetical resources of a diocese, e.g. persons competent in scripture, theology, education etc.

4. A fundamental rethinking on the nature and essence of minis-

try ought to take place. This is primarily a theological issue but one which has major educational implications. The existence of other ministries, apart from priestly ministry, deserves to be acknowledged and their development encouraged.

5. Following from, and linked to, No 4 above is the need to re-examine the present formation structures available to those who will be involved in Christian ministry. It is inconceivable that those chosen by God to minister in his Church in a priestly capacity should be trained in an environment which is totally removed from the communities in which they will serve. Similarly it is inconceivable that the training of adults for involvement in other ecclesial ministries should be carried out in a random manner and one which is not related in any way to the formation of candidates for priestly ministry (with whom they will later work).

6. Unlike the corpus of ecclesiastical laws which the 1983 Code of Canon Law replaced, the new code remains silent on the question of conducting theological studies for clerics in isolation from similar courses of study for lay persons. Thus, to be of mutual benefit, courses of theological studies in Pontifical Universities for clerics and non-clerics ought to be held in common. This may provide the beginning of the realisation of the recommendations in No 5 above.

7. The training of secondary school catechists deserves to be re-examined. The possession of a degree in theology and a higher diploma in education is hardly sufficient, on its own, to give competence in modern catechetical theory and methodology. Catechesis involves learning on multi-dimensional levels – levels that greatly surpass educational methodologies employed in classrooms to teach secular subjects.

8. More university centres (or departments) of catechetics should be established. These centres ought to work in close collaboration with existing departments of education, continuing education and theology.

9. Greater care will have to be taken in the selection and training of those who will work as adult catechists.

10. As with all recommendations which call for the setting up of new structures and positions of responsibility, the question of resources will have to be addressed i.e. who will finance the training of adult catechists and who will pay their wages? Here the

answer lies less in asking where additional funds will come from than in restructuring present diocesan finances in accordance with where needs are greatest. The very considerable investment in primary and second level schooling, together with the overall financial commitments of each diocese, may have to be re-examined on a more cost-effective basis.

11. A more comprehensive understanding of adulthood, adult learning and the educational needs of the adult must be developed within the Irish context.

12. Most importantly of all, a visible and genuine commitment by clergy and religious to the field of adult catechesis must be encouraged as a matter of priority.

General Conclusion

We have arrived at the end of a work which set out to examine the theme of Christian faith in a changing Irish society. We have seen that, in any society, for Christian faith to flourish and pass from generation to generation an appropriate and adequate system of Christian education (catechesis) must be in place. The universal catechetical methodology in existence prior to Vatican II was that of Christian education as doctrinal transmission.

This particular model of Christian education had been in place for almost four hundred years – since its inception at the Council of Trent [1545-1563]. The effectiveness of the catechism (the primary educational method of this catechetical system) can not be doubted. However, for the greater part of the history of the catechism its doctrinal statements echoed in the ears of peoples across the world who already possessed a strong faith commitment to those truths of Christianity inherited from a vibrant local Christian community.

As the present century progressed the social conditions changed significantly and the dogmas of Christian faith had begun to fall from the catechism onto newer generations of Christians whose inherent faith was no longer automatically capable of their assimilation. The catechism approach began to fail precisely because the social conditions out of which it grew (a vibrant evangelical and missionary Church anxious to proclaim and defend its truths) no longer existed.

The Second Vatican Council [1962-1965], anxious to discern how the Church ought to adapt for a third millenium of Christianity, spent most of its sittings deliberating what might best be termed the 'basics': the Church's understanding of itself and its vision for the future. The topic of catechesis was introduced briefly at the Council but the main task of working out definitive statements on the subject was left to post-conciliar commissions. The most striking result in the post-conciliar era was the re-introduction of an adapted form of the adult catechumenate of the early Church.

CONCLUSION

In re-introducing the adult catechumenate (the R.C.I.A) the Church returned adult catechesis to the centre stage which it held once before – 'adult catechesis is the chief form of catechesis, towards which all other catechesis is directed'. The restoration has also had major ecclesiological and theological implications which have yet to be worked out.

I have strongly suggested that the R.C.I.A. may offer the most promising approach to catechesis in Ireland today. The catechetical model implicit in this rite is that of Christian education as ongoing initiation – initiation (of both minors and adults) into an adult faith community. It is obvious, then, that for the model to work effectively a strong local adult Church is essential. The key word used in the rite is that of 'adapt'. This work made some suggestions as to how it might be adapted to the Irish context and what implications it would have for Christian education in this country.

Perhaps the single greatest challenge to Christian faith in Ireland today lies in a critical re-examination of the continuing dependence of the Irish Church on the primary and secondary school systems as a sole means of introducing Christian values and a Christian way of life to Irish youth. I have questioned this practice on two levels: firstly, on the level that Christian education received in one's school years can never be fully adequate for all of later adult life and, secondly, that the undisputed effectiveness of the Catholic school in the past was in great measure due to the faith and prayer of the home and to the pervasive influence of the faith in the parish community and, indeed, throughout the national community at large (none of which can be taken for granted to exist today).

I am not, by any means, implying that the focus of Christian education in Ireland today should move away from the school and be located instead in the home, the parish and the adult community. That, I believe, would be an unwarranted and a dangerously mistaken conclusion. What evidence and experience do indicate is that the school ought not be left as the only or even as the primary focus of Christian education and faith formation. The school ought not be left to carry the responsibility of catechesis on its own. The isolation of the school in the catechetical domain must be ended. The 1971 *General Catechetical Directory*, the 1977 Synod and its concluding document, *Catechesi Tradendae*, emphasise the primary and fundamental role of the home, parents and the family in the handing on of faith. These documents stress the indispensable *locus* of the parish community as the place where young people are initiated into an adult Christian faith and life and are helped to grow towards Christian maturity.

It is interesting to note that for catechesis, as for many aspects of life, the way forward is often steeped in past traditions. The task of interpreting the past to assist the future is an ongoing one. This is particularly true in the case of the R.C.I.A. which offers a catechetical model for use in keeping the faith in contemporary Ireland. In the words of T.S. Eliot:

> We shall not cease from exploration
> And the end of our exploration
> Shall be to arrive where we started
> And know the place for the first time.
>
> (*Choruses* from 'The Rock')

Notes

CHAPTER I

1. Ray Brady, 'Will Our Children Believe and Belong?', *The Furrow*, 41:1 (1990), 4.

2. Máire NicGhiolla Phádraig, *A Survey of Religious Attitudes and Beliefs, 1973-74*, 4 Vols (Research and Development Report 1975). Also her Ph.D. Dissertation based upon the above research, U.C.D., 1981. A condensed version of her research is available in 'Religion in Ireland: A Preliminary Analysis', *Social Studies*, 5:2 (1976), 113-180.

3. Micheál MacGréil, 'Religious Beliefs and Practice of Dublin Adults', *Social Studies*, 3:2 (1974).

4. K.P. O'Doherty, 'Adaption to Religious Values: A Study of University Students', *Social Studies*, 3:2 (1974).

5. Thomas Inglis, 'How Religious are Irish University Students?' Research and Development Report 1979.

6. Bernadette McMahon, 'A Study of Religion Among Catholic Adolescents Attending Some Dublin Schools', Research and Development Report 1981.

7. Brigid Reynolds/Sean J. Healy, *Social Analysis in the Light of the Gospel*, Dublin: Justice Office, 1983.

8. Ann Breslin, 'A Survey of Religious, Moral and Civic Values of Senior School-goers', Research and Development Unit, Maynooth, 1983.

9. Micheál MacGréil, *Religious Practice and Attitudes in Ireland: Report of a Survey of Religious Attitudes and Practice and Related Issues in the Republic of Ireland 1988-1989*, Report published by the Survey and Research Unit, Department of Social Studies, St Patrick's College, Maynooth, 1991.

10. Michael Paul Gallagher, *The Furrow*, 25 (1974), 186. The same article was reprinted in *Struggles of Faith*, Dublin: Columba Press, 1990, 10.

11. Michael Paul Gallagher, 'What hope for Irish faith?', *The Furrow*, 1978. Also in *Struggles of Faith*, 18.

12. Michael Paul Gallagher, *The Furrow*, 25 (1974), 188.

13. *The Furrow*, 29 (1978) and *Struggles of Faith*, 17.

14. Bernadette McMahon, *A Study of Religion Among Catholic Adolescents Attending Some Dublin Schools*, Research and Development Report 1981.

15. Michael Paul Gallagher, *Help my Unbelief*, Dublin: Veritas, 1983, 35.

16. Liam Ryan, 'Faith under Survey', *The Furrow*, 34:1 (1983), 4.

17. Ibid., 5.

18. Ibid., 6.

19. Ibid., 7.

20. Ibid., 6.

21. Peadar Kirby, *Is Irish Catholicism Dying? Liberating an Imprisoned Church*, Dublin: Mercier Press, 1984.

22. Ibid., 41.

23. Niall O'Brien, *The Furrow*, February 1984.

24. Kirby, op cit, 34.

25. Quoted by Kirby, op cit, 32.

26. Seán Healy/Brigid Reynolds, *Ireland Today: Reflections in the Light of the Gospel*, Dublin: Justice Office, 1985. Compiled from p 95, footnote 37.

27. Liam Ryan, 'Faith under Survey', *The Furrow*, 34:1 (1983), 5.

28. Statistics in this paragraph are drawn from Ann Breslin and John Weafer, *Religious Beliefs, Practice and Moral Attitudes: A Comparison of Two Irish Surveys*, Council for Research and Development, 1985.

29. Máire NicGhiolla Phádraig, 'Religious Practice and Secularization', in *Ireland: a Sociological Profile*, Patrick Clancy et al., Dublin: IPA, 1986, 149.

30. Micheál MacGréil 1990 survey.

31. Ibid., 10.

32. Ibid., 21.

33. Ibid., 19.

34. See John H. Westerholl, *Will Our Children Have Faith?*, New York: Seabury Press, 1976.

35. Kevin Nichols, 'Religion as a Classroom Subject', *Orientations*, Slough: St Paul Publications, 1979, 49.

36. Among others, see Seán Freyne, 'Religious Education at Third Level', *Irish Catechist*, 7:1 (1983); Pat Fitzgerald, 'Religious Education in a Regional Technical College', *Irish Catechist*, 7:1 (1983), 9-10; Fergal O'Connor, 'Religion in Irish Universities', *Doctrine and Life*, 17 (1967), 186-191; James Good, 'The Priest in Education', *Christus Rex*, 24 (1970), 75-82.

37. The works of Piaget, Kohlberg, Gagne, Goldman and Fowler in the areas of cognitive development, moral development, learning theories, and faith development have made a significant contribution to the whole area of religious education today.

38. *Children of God* series. Introduction to Teacher's Handbook, 'Walk in my Presence', 9.

39. Ibid., 12.

40. *cf* Richard Reichert, *A Learning Process for Religious Education*, Dayton, Ohio: Pflaum, 1975, 80.

41. *Children of God* series. Introduction to Teacher's Handbook, 'Walk in my Presence', 9.

42. *cf* Berard Marthaler, 'Socialization as a Model for Catechetics', in Padraic O'Hare (ed.), *Foundations of Religious Education*, New York: Paulist Press, 1978.

43. *cf* Desmond Murtagh, 'Will Our Children Have Faith?', *The Furrow*, 42:4 (1991), 221-226.

44. *eg.* Nicholas A. Casey, 'Short Ladder to Nowhere: The Crisis in Senior Religion', *The Furrow*, 35:2 (1984), 103-108. The extent of the 'crisis' is well documented in John A. Weafer/Ann M. Hanley, *Whither Religious Education? A Survey of post-primary teachers in Ireland, with commentaries edited by Dermot A. Lane*, Dublin: Columba Press, 1991. The need for a concrete philosophy of Catholic Education is more evident now than ever. *cf* Demot Lane, *Catholic Education and the School: Some theological reflections*, Dublin: Veritas, 1991.

45. Desmond Murtagh, op cit, 224. This claim is statistically validated by the Weafer/Hanley survey above.

46. Weafer/Hanley, op cit.

47. Irish Episcopal Commission for Catechetics, *A Syllabus for the Religious Education of Pupils in Post-Primary Schools*, Dublin: Veritas, 1982, 9.

48. Ibid., 4.

49. Ibid., 4.

50. Ibid, 79.

51. Ibid., 8.

52. Nicholas Casey, 'Short Ladder to Nowhere: The Crisis in Senior Religion', *The Furrow*, 35:2 (1984), 101.

53. Irene Ní Mháille, 'A Ladder with Nothing to Stand On', *The Furrow*, 35:7 (1984), 454.

54. Tony Hanna, 'The Catholic Youth: An Endangered Species', *The Furrow*, 38:2 (1987), 84.

55. Catechetical Association of Ireland, 'C.A.I. Survey on Religious Studies as a Subject for Leaving Certificate', *Irish Catechist*, 2:1 (1978), 14-23.

56. The situation in Northern Ireland, where Religious Studies is part of the school curriculum and, as such, is examinable by the State, is discussed in Sean McIlroy, 'R.E. as an Exam Subject', *Irish Catechist*, 5:4 (1981), 4-12.

57. Brian Kelly, 'Religion as a Leaving Cert Subject', *Irish Catechist*, 2:1 (1978), 24.

58. Ibid., 27.

59. *cf* John Weafer, 'Vocations: A Review of National and International Trends', *The Furrow*, August 1988, 501-511.

60. *cf* Jeremiah Newman/Liam Ryan/Conor K. Ward, 'Attitudes of Young People towards Vocations', *Social Studies*, 1:5 (1972), 531-550.

61. Micheál MacGréil, 1990 Survey, 43.

62. Recognising the universal priesthood of the baptised does not, by any means, take from the presbyteral priesthood. From the Middle Ages, the latter was the only 'recognised' priesthood. Today, theological debate on the subject of priesthood falls within two categories: those who draw a clear distinction between the two and those who see little or none. Recent material which argues in favour of the distinction between the universal priesthood of the baptised and sacerdotalist priesthood include: B. D. Marlianges, *Clés pour une theologie du ministère*, Paris, 1978; M. Thurian, *Priesthood and Ministry, Ecumenical Research*, London, 1983; J. Galot, *Theology of the Priesthood*, San Francisco, 1979; T.F. O'Meara, *Theology for Ministry*, Wilmington, Delaware, 1983. Material which argues against such a distinction include: Edward Schillebeecks, *Ministry: A Case for Change*, London, 1985; Edward Schillebeecks, *The Church with a Human Face: A New and Expanded Theology of Ministry*, London, 1985; Hans Küng, *Why Priests?*, London, 1972.

63. Michael Warren, 'The Catechumen in the Kitchen' in Dermot Lane (ed.), *Religious Education and the Future: Essays in Honour of Patrick Wallace*, Dublin: Columba Press, 1986, 80.

64. Laurence Ryan, 'Is there a shortage of priests?', *The Furrow*, 39:10 (1988), 619-626.

65. For a succinct history of priesthood, see Aidan Nichols, *Holy Order: Apostolic Priesthood from the New Testament to the Second Vatican Council*, Dublin: Veritas, 1990.

CHAPTER II

1. W. M. Abbott (ed.), *The Documents of Vatican II*, London: Geoffrey Chapman, 1966, 715.

2. The relevant preparatory documents of Vatican II are included in the *Acta et Documenta*, Rome: Vatican City Press, esp. series 1, Vols. 2-4.

3. *Acta et Documenta* I, vol. 11.

4. *Christus Dominus*, 44. *cf* A. Flannery, *Vatican II: The Conciliar and Post-Conciliar Documents*, Dublin: Dominican Publications, 1981, 590.

5. For an historical overview of the fate of this schemata on catechetics at Vatican II see the introduction to Bernard Marthaler's *Catechetics in Context: Notes and Commentary on the General Catechetical Directory*, Huntington, Indiana: Our Sunday Visitor, 1972, xvi - xxi.

6. *Ad Gentes*, 20. *cf* Flannery, op cit, 836.

7. *Christus Dominus*, 12 (*cf* Flannery, op cit, 575) also *De Ecclesia*, 25.

8. *Dei Verbum*, 25. *cf* Flannery, op cit, 764.

9. On this point see Michael Donnellan 'Bishops and Uniformity in Religious Education: Vatican I to Vatican II' in Michael Warren (ed.), *Sourcebook for Modern Catechetics*, Winona, Minnesota: Saint Mary's Press, 1983, 243, footnote 19.

10. Ibid., article 44. *cf* Flannery, op cit, 590.

11. Introduction to the *Decree on Christian Education*. *cf* Flannery, op cit, 726.

12. Promulgated on November 21st, 1964. See Austin Flannery (ed.), *Vatican II, The Conciliar and Post Conciliar Documents*, Dublin: Dominican Publications, 1981, 350.

13. Gregory Baum, *Commentary on the Constitution of the Church of Vatican II*, New York: Deus Books / Paulist Press, 1967, 23.

14. *Lumen Gentium*. See English translation in A. Flannery, op. cit., 358.

15. Ibid., article 10, 361.

16. Ibid., article 16, 367.

17. Ibid., article 16, 367.

18. Gregory Baum, *Commentary on the Constitution of the Church of Vatican Council II*, New York: Paulist Press, 1964, 38.

19. *cf* Flannery, op cit, article 31, 388-9.

20. Ibid., article 32, 390.

21. Ibid., article 13.

22. Ibid., article 14.

23. Ibid., articles 11 and 30.

24. Ibid., article 5.

25. Ibid., article 6.

26. Ibid., article 19.

27. Ibid., article 6.
28. Ibid., article 4.
29. Ibid., articles 24-25.
30. Ibid., article 14.
31. Ibid., articles 14, 15, 17, 19 and 26.
32. On this point see William J. Bausch, 'The Role of the Sacraments in the Formation of Faith', *Living Light* 14 (1977), 294-311.
33. See Aidan Kavanagh, *The Shape of Baptism: The Rite of Christian Initiation*, New York: Paulist Press, 1978.
34. Eugene Kennedy, *Believing*, New York: Doubleday, 1974, 40.
35. Acts 2:22-39.
36. John H. Westerhoff, III, *Will our Children have Faith?* New York: Seabury Press, 1976, 44.
37. Bernard Cooke, 'Living Liturgy: Life as Liturgy' in Gloria Duka & Joanmarie Smith (eds.), *Emerging Issues in Religious Education*, New York: Paulist Press, 1976, 116.
38. *cf* especially the Dogmatic Constitution on the Church, *Lumen Gentium*, articles 30ff in Flannery, op cit, 388ff.
39. Ibid., article 14.
40. Edward Schillebeeckx, *Vatican II: The Real Achievement*, London: Sheed & Ward, 1966, 27-28.
41. W. M. Abbott (ed.), *The Documents of Vatican II*, London: Chapman, 1966, 133-134.
42. Jacques Bournique, 'Catechetics after the Council' in *Presenting the Christian Message to Africa*, London: Geoffrey Chapman, 1965, 118.
43. *The Constitution on the Liturgy*, article 14. *cf* Flannery, op cit, 7-8.
44. *Constitution on the Sacred Liturgy*, article 10. *cf* Flannery, op cit, 6.
45. Instruction on the *Constitution on the Sacred Liturgy*, article 7.
46. Johannes Hoffinger, 'The Evangelising Power of the Liturgy', *Worship* 28 (1954), 38-357.
47. *Constitution on the Sacred Liturgy*, article 10. *cf* Flannery, op cit, 6.
48. Instruction on the *Constitution on the Liturgy* article 5. *cf* Flannery op cit, 46.
49. *Constitution on the Sacred Liturgy* article 35 (2). *cf* Flannery, op cit, 12.
50. *Constitution on the Sacred Liturgy* article 52. *cf* Flannery, op cit, 17-18.
51. Instruction on the *Constitution on the Liturgy* article 6. *cf* Flannery, op cit, 46.
52. *Acta Apostolicae Sedis* [the Vatican gazette, published a varying number of times each year. It carries the original text of the more important Vatican documents], 54 (May 30, 1962), 310-311.

53. *Acta Apostolicae Sedis* 59 (1966), No. 14, 722. cf Abbot, op cit, 600-601.
54. *Acta Apostolicae Sedis* 56 (1964), No. 41, 111. cf Abbot, op cit, 152.
55. *Acta Apostolicae Sedis* 58 (1966), No. 6, 1001. cf Abbot, op cit, 545.
56. *Acta Apostolicae Sedis* 58 (1966), 963. cf Abbot, op cit, 601.
57. *Acta Apostolicae Sedis* 58 (1966), 962. cf Abbot, op cit, 600.
58. *Acta Apostolicae Sedis* 58 (1966), 1001. cf Abbot, op cit, 545.
59. *Acta Apostolicae Sedis* 56 (1964), 115. cf Abbot, op cit. 155.
60. Ibid., 118. cf Abbot, op cit, 156-57.
61. *Acta Apostolicae Sedis* 58 (1966), 963. cf Abbot, op cit, 601.
62. *Acta Apostolicae Sedis* 58 (1966), 962. cf Abbot, op cit. 600.

CHAPTER III

1. For text of the *General Catechetical Directory* see Austin Flannery (ed.), *Vatican II: More Postconciliar Documents*, Dublin: Dominican Publications, 1982, 529-606.

2. For documentation on the six International Catechetical Study Weeks see Part I of Michael Warren (ed.), *Sourcebook for Modern Catechetics*, Winona, Minnesota: St. Mary's Press, 1983 and especially Luis Erdozain, 'The Evolution of Catechetics: A Survey of Six International Study Weeks on Catechetics', *Lumen Vitae* 25 (1970), 7-31.

3. L. Erdozain has surveyed the contributions made by these study weeks in a useful article, 'The Evolution of Catechesis', in *Lumen Vitae*, 25 (1970), 1-31.

4. D. S. Amalorpvadass, *International Catechetical Congress: Selected Documentation*, 134.

5. cf G. Caprile, *Civilta Cattolica*, (n. 2906), July 17, 1971, 170. Cardinal Wright made much the same point in his news conference, cf *L'Osservatore Romano*, June 18, 1971.

6. *La rivista del catechismo*, 8 (July-August, 1971), 272. The editorial note claiming authorship and explaining the nature of the document is signed G.B.B., presumbly Giam Battishta Belloli, the editor of the review.

7. *General Catechetical Directory*, pars. 24, 97.

8. Karl Rahner, (ed)., *Sacramentum Mundi*, I:117.

9. *General Catechetical Directory*, par. 38.

10. *General Catechetical Directory*, par. 36.

11. *General Catechetical Directory*, par. 112.

12. *General Catechetical Directory*, par. 20.

13. D.S. Amalorpvadass, *International Catechetical Congress (ICC), Selected Documentation*, 54-55.

14. *The Decree on the Apostolate of the Laity, Apostolicam Actuositatem*, par. 9.

15. *ICC, Selected Documentation*, 124.

16. *General Catechetical Directory*, pars. 75&79.

17. Johannes Hoffinger (ed.), *Teaching All Nations*, (A Symposium on Modern Catechetics), Freiburg: Herder, 1961, 388. Eichstatt formulated a series of specific proposals, many of which have since been implemented by Vatican II and the Congregation for Divine Worship, cf 392-393.

18. *ICC Selected Documentation*, 42.

19. *The Decree on the Life and Ministry of Priests, Presbyterorum Ordinis*, par. 6.

20. *General Catechetical Directory*, par. 65.

21. *Lumen Gentium*, par. 9.

22. *General Catechetical Directory*, par. 13.

23. Ibid., par. 33.

24. Ibid., par. 34.

25. Ibid., par. 37. The Third International Study Week at Bangkok in 1962 emphasised *adaptation*, 'by developing the doctrine (of Christ) according to analogies, images or forms of expression familiar to the people of a given region or culture'. *cf* Nebreda in *Lumen Vitae*, 27 (1962), 727.

26. *General Catechetical Directory*, par. 36.

27. Ibid., par. 34.

28. *Decree on the Church's Missionary Activity, Ad Gentes*, par. 13.

29. Ibid., pars. 13-14. These paragraphs summarise key aspects of the conciliar vision of Christian Initiation.

30. *Constitution on the Church, Lumen Gentium* par. 14.

31. *Christus Dominus*, par. 14.

32. *Ad Gentes*, par. 14.

33. The idea of faith as a developing reality is one which was made known primarily by James Fowler. His work is based on Piaget's theories of cognitive development. *cf* James Fowler, 'Stages in Faith: The Structural Development Approach', in *Values and Moral Development*. Thomas C. Hennessy (ed.), New York: Paulist Press, 1976.

34. *Rite of Christian Initiation of Adults*, par. 1.

35. Ralph Keifer, 'Christian Initiation: The State of the Question', *Worship*, 48 (September, 1974), 395.

36. Michel Dujarier, 'Sponsorship', *Concilium* 1 (Feb. 1967), 29.

37. *Rite of Christian Initiation of Adults*, par. 19:1.

38. *Rite of Christian Initiation of Adults*, par. 19:4.

39. Ibid., pars. 22-24.

40. Ibid., par. 21.

41. Ibid., par. 25.

42. Ibid., pars. 22&139.

43. The meaning of exorcism used here can be found in Balthasar Fischer, 'Exorcism in the Catholic Baptism Rites after Vatican II', *Studia Liturgica*, 10 (1974), 48-55.

44. *Rite of Christian Initiation of Adults*, par. 25:1&2.

45. Aidan. Kavanagh, 'The Norm of Baptism: The Rite of Christian Initiation of Adults', *Worship*, 48:3 (1974), 147.

CHAPTER IV

1. Donal Murray, 'The Roman Synod', *Irish Catechist*, 1:3 (1977) 28.
2. Ibid., p. 29.
3. Ibid., p. 39.
4. *Documents of the Fifth Synod of Bishops, Rome 1977*, Dublin: Veritas Publications, 1977,8.
5. Ibid., p. 13/14.
6. Ibid., p. 19.
7. Ibid., p. 19.
8. Ibid., p. 20.
9. Ibid., p. 21.
10. Paul Lebeau/Ian Charytonski, 'The Fifth Synod of Bishops and the Church's Catechetical Mission', *Lumen Vitae* 33 (1978), 20.
11. For example that associated with the Dutch Catechism for Adults. *cf A New Catechism* commissioned by the Dutch Hierarchy, New York: Herder, 1967. For discussion of the document see Michael Donnellan, 'The German and Dutch Catechisms in Retrospect', *The Living Light* 12 (1975), 20-29.
12. Quoted by Francis J. Butler, *Lumen Vitae*, 32 (1977), 497.
13. *cf* Canon 759.
14. *cf* Canon 762.
15. 1917 *Code of Canon Law*, Canon 1342 n. 2.
16. *Sacrosanctum Concilium*, April 3, 1971, n. 42.
17. See *Christus Dominus* n. 14 and the *General Catechetical Directory* n. 17.
18. See *Lumen Gentium* 12, 35 and *Catechesi Tradendae* 16.
19. Canon 827, n. 1.
20. *Catechesi Tradendae*, par. 50.
21. *Christus Dominus*, par. 14.
22. *Inter Mirifica*, par. 16.
23. *Catechesi Tradendae*, pars. 45-50.
24. Canon 781.
25. Canons 783 and 790.
26. Canon 784.
27. See *Ad Gentes*, pars. 13-14.
28. Ibid., par. 38.
29. Canon 793 n. 2.
30. *Catechesi Tradendae*, par. 5.
31. Ibid., par. 23.

32. Ibid., par. 48.

33. Ibid., par. 20.

34. Ibid., par. 21.

35. Ibid., par. 55.

36. Ibid., pars. 119&134.

37. Joseph Ratzinger, 'Sources and Transmission of the Faith', *Communio*, 10 (1983), 18.

38. Waltar Kasper, 'The Church's Profession of Faith: On Drafting a New Catholic Catechism for Adults', *Communio*, 11 (1984), 29, 57.

39. *Origins*, December 19, 1985, 448.

40. *Origins* NC Documentary Service, December 19 1985, 452.

41. Ibid., December 9, 1985, 6. A comprehensive account and evaluation of the 1985 Synod can be found in Giuseppe Alberigo/James Provost (eds.), 'Synod 1985: An Evaluation', *Concilium* No. 188, Edinburgh: T & T Clark, 1986.

42. *cf* Joseph Ratzinger, 'On Route toward a Universal Catechism: Progress Report', *Living Light*, 24:2 (1988), 152-155. A provisional *sub secreto* text of the proposed Universal Catechism was sent to all of the Church's bishops in 1989. *cf Catechism for the Universal Church: Provisional Text*, Vatican City: Vatican Press, 1989. In Ireland nine bishops drew up recommendations on the draft text on behalf of the Irish Episcopal Conference. During the June 1990 Episcopal Meeting in Maynooth the bishops presented their report. In brief, the bishops were not happy with the contents. They expressed concern that much of the contents lacked the richness of the vision of Vatican II and offered fifteen pages of recommendations on how the text might be improved.

43. Johann-Baptist Metz/Edward Schillebeeckx, 'World Catechism or Incultuation', *Concilium* No. 204, Edinburgh: T & T Clark Ltd., 1989.

44. Sacred Congregation for the Doctrine of the Faith, *Catechism for the Universal Church*, Vatican City: Libreria Editrice Vaticana, 1989.

45. The confidential recommendations of the Irish Episcopal Conference on the draft document were kindly made available to me.

CHAPTER V

1. Working Party established by the Adult Education Commission, *Adults and Education: A Survey 1982-1983* , Dublin: 1983.

2. Ibid., 156.

3. Ibid., 166.

4. Micheál MacGréil, *Education Participation in Ireland*, Survey and Research Unit, Department of Social Studies, St Patrick's College, Maynooth, February, 1990, 11.

5. Ibid., 12.

6. Department of Education, *Curaclaim na Bunscoile*, Dublin: Government Publications, 1971.

7. Department of Education, *Rules and Programmes for Secondary Schools*, Dublin: Government Publications, 1972.

8. Department of Education, *White Paper on Educational Development*, Dublin: Government Publications, 1980.

9. Department of Education, *Programme for Action in Education 1984-1987*, Dublin: Government Publications, 1984.

10. Con Murphy, *National Education Survey: Interim Report*, Prl. 1343, Dublin: Stationary Office, 1971.

11. Con Murphy, *Adult Education in Ireland*, Dublin: Stationary Office, 1973. Prl. 3465.

12. Micheál MacGréil, op cit, 10.

13. Con Murphy, op cit.

14. Department of Education, *White Paper on Educational Development (1980): Adult Education*, Dublin: Government Publications, 1980.

15. Commission on Adult Education, *Lifelong Learning: Report of the Commission on Adult Education* , Dublin: Stationary Office, 1983.

16. Ibid., 9.

17. Ibid., 24.

18. Ibid., 52.

19. Curriculum and Examinations Board, *Issues and Structures in Education: A Consultative Document*, Dublin: Government Publications, September, 1984.

20. Ibid., 13.

21. Department of Education, *Programme for Action in Education 1984–1987*, Government Publications, 1984, 5.2 and 5.6.

22. Ibid., 1.1, 6.5 and 6.19.

23. Mater Dei Academic Staff, 'Programme for Action in Education 1984-1987: A Response'. Published in *The Furrow*, 35:10 (1984), 639-647. Here p. 641 is quoted.

24. *cf* Liam Carey, 'Adult Religious Education', *The Irish Catechist*, 1

(1977), 48-57.

25. cf Enid Cuddy, 'Limerick's Adult Education Institute' *Reality*, 39:2 (1975), 10-13.

26. Bishop Peter Birch, 'Kilkenny's Adult Education Centre', *Reality*, 39:5 (1975), 24.

27. Ibid., 27.

28. Ibid., 29.

29. Liam Carey, 'Adult Religious Education', *The Irish Catechist*, 1 (1977), 55.

30. Joseph McCann, 'Adult Religious Education - why a faith community is not yet being built', *Irish Catechist*, 7:4 (1983), 4.

31. Liam Carey, op cit, 55.

32. Liam Lacey, 'Adult Catechesis in Ireland: A Way Forward', *Irish Catechist*, 7:3 (1983), 36.

33. Liam Carey, 'Discussion Groups in Adult R.E.', *Irish Catechist*, 5:3 (1981), 4-5.

34. Peter Boucher, *Adult Religious Education - How? Needs, Objectives and Methods*. An M.A. thesis submitted to the Department of Adult and Continuing Education at the University of Ulster, Magee College, 1987, 13. See also his article 'Religious Education', *Intercom*, November, 1990, 12-13.

35. Peter Boucher, M.A. Thesis, 1987.

36. For a contemporary understanding of Adult Education see, among others, Gabriel Moran, *Education Towards Adulthood. Religion and Lifelong Learning*, Dublin: Gill and Macmillan, 1980; Padraic O'Hare, *Foundations of Religious Education*, New York: Paulist Press, 1978.

37. Briege O'Hare, 'Parish Catechesis', *Irish Catechist*, 5:3 (1981), 11-15.

38. Briege O' Hare, art. cit., 13.

39. cf Wim Saris, *Towards a Living Church: Family and Community Catechesis*, London: Collins, 1980.

40. Brendan Quinlan, 'Adult Catechesis in the Parish', *Irish Catechist*, 8:2 (1984), 23.

41. *Directory of Adult Religious Education in Ireland*, Dublin: Veritas, 1985. Foreward by Ted Fleming of the Institute of Religious Education, Mount Oliver, Dundalk, Co. Louth.

42. Gene Trester, 'Adult Biblical Education', *Intercom*, March 1991, 24-25. In this connection I would like to express my gratitude to Dr Fergus O'Ferrall of the National Bible Society of Ireland for making me aware of the impressive developments in the area of adult biblical education in Ireland over the recent past.

43. Tom Cooney, 'Parish Cells', *Intercom*, December 1990, 14-15.

44. Sile O'Reilly, 'The Parish Catechist', *Intercom*, July 1990, 12-13.

45. Betty Maher, 'Hospital Chaplaincy', *Intercom*, September 1990, 13-14.

46. Bishop of Cloyne, Lenten Pastoral, 1968; Bishop of Kildare, Lenten Pastoral, 1970; Bishop of Cork & Ross, Lenten Pastoral, 1982; Bishop of Galway, Lenten Pastoral, 1972; Bishop of Elphin, Lenten Pastoral, 1987; Bishop of Achonry; Lenten Pastoral, 1987; Bishop of Kerry, Lenten Pastoral, 1979, etc, etc.

47. Bishop of Achonry, Lenten Pastorals 1982 & 1984; Bishop of Kerry, Lenten Pastoral, 1977; Bishop of Galway, Lenten Pastoral, 1972; Bishop of Cloyne, Lenten Pastoral, 1977, etc., etc.

48. Bishop of Cloyne, Lenten Pastoral, 1969; Bishop of Kildare, Lenten Pastoral, 1975; Bishop of Kerry, Lenten Pastoral, 1981, etc. etc.

49. *cf*, for example, Bishop of Cork, *Diocesan Programme of Catechetical Instruction 1962-1963* dealing with 'the precepts of the Church', 'sin and temptation' as well as 'works of mercy' and the same bishop's *Diocesan Programme of Catechetical Instruction 1964-65* on the topic of 'our faith'. In both of these programmes a list was given of the topics that were to be preached upon on particular Sundays of the year and what was to be said about them.

50. Bishop of Achonry, Lenten Pastoral, 1991.

51. Bishop of Kerry, Lenten Pastoral, 1982.

52. Archbishop of Dublin, Christmas Message, 1991, *Come Home for Christmas*.

53. Bishop of Clogher, Lent, 1986, *Christian Renewal. cf* also Bishop of Kerry, Kerry Diocesan Assembly, October, 1982 where the key problem of people having an inadequate understanding of the nature of the Church and of their role in it is presented.

54. Bishop of Achonry, Lenten Pastoral, 1987.

55. Donal Murray, *A Special Concern, The Philosophy of Education: a Christian Perspective*, Dublin: Veritas, 1991, 12.

56. *Catechesi Tradendae*, par. 43.

57. *cf* Bishop Michael Murphy, *The Parish: The Challenge Ahead*, Cork: The Printing House, 1986, 3.

58. Bishop of Elphin, Private Letter to the Priests of the Diocese, 1982.

59. Bishop of Kerry, Kerry Diocesan Assembly, 24th-29th October, 1982, 35-36. Unpublished Document for private circulation.

60. *cf* Gerard Clifford, Archdiocese of Armagh, *Pastoral Directory for the Priest*, Lurgan: Ronan Press Ltd., 1984, 71 ff.

61. *cf* Address by Bishop Murphy on Saturday, June 11th, 1988 to the Federation of Christian Brothers and other Catholic Primary Schools Parents Councils.

62. Bishop of Clogher, Lenten Pastoral, 1986, *Christian Renewal*.

63. Based on information made available by the respective Irish diocesan offices.

64. Donal Murrray, *A Special Concern, The Philosophy of Education: A Christian Perspective*, Dublin: Veritas, 1991.

65. Ibid., 3.

66. Bishop of Cork, Talk at Opening of Adult Religious Education Course in Ballincollig, Sept 13th, 1988.

CHAPTER VI

1. Michael Tynan, *Catholic Instruction in Ireland 1720-1950*, Dublin: Four Court's Press, 1985, 9.

2. Louis J. Puhl, *The Spiritual Exercises of St Ignatius*, Chicago: Loyola University Press, 1951, 158, par 361. 9.

3. Louis J. Puhl, ibid., 159 par. 363. 11.

4. An Act to make further provisions with respect to University Education in Ireland. 1st August, 1908 from the *Public General Acts, 8th Year of the Reign of Edward VII*, London: H.M. Stationary Office, 1908.

5. The degree studied for by clerics is that of Batchelor of Divinity, B.D. The degree awarded to lay people is that of Batchelor of Arts in Theology, B.A. (Theol.)

6. Louis J. Puhl. op cit, 160, par. 365. 13.

7. John McHugh and Charles Callen (eds)., *Catechism of the Council of Trent for Parish Priests*, New York: Wagner, 1923, 11.

8. William F. Murphy, *Anthropological Catechesis - the adoption of the anthropological method in catechesis studied from a theological viewpoint*. An Unpublished Doctoral Thesis submitted to the Pontificia Universitas Gregoriana, Rome, 1973, xvi.

9. Gabriel Moran, *God Still Speaks: The Basis of Christian Education*, London: Search Press, 1970, 21.

10. Joseph Jungman, *The Good News Yesterday and Today*, New York: Sadlier, 1962.

11. *General Catechetical Directory* par. 10. cf Flannery, op cit, 537.

12. *Catechesi Tradendae*, par. 16 in Austin Flannery, op cit, 771.

13. For a succinct treatment of the difficulty encountered in dealing with the languages involved in catechesis see Ulrich Hemel, 'Religious Education, Catechesis, Evngelisation: some terminological difficulties at an international level', *The Irish Catechist*, 9:1 (1985), 4-17.

14. Gabriel Moran, *Vision and Tactics: Towards an Adult Church*, London: Burns & Oates, 1970, 15.

15. Avery Dulles, *Models of the Church*, Dublin: Gill and Macmillan, 1976.

16. Avery Dulles, ibid., 8.

17. Ibid., 27.

18. Vatican II mandated the restoration of the Ancient Catechumenate in the Decree *Sacrosanctum Concilium* which was promulgated on December 4th., 1963. cf pars. 64-66 and 69.

19. The ancient catechumenate did not die but found its way into seminaries and houses of religious formation. This thesis is put forward by several theologians and is, today, being investigated in relation to its possible usage in contemporary seminaries and houses of formation. cf Charles E. Bouchard, 'Initial Religious Formation as an Extension of the New Rite of Initiation of Adults', in *Review for Religious*, 36:4 (1977), 592-

599 and Eugene Duffy, 'Seminary Formation', *The Furrow*, 40:8 (1989), 451-460.

20. Charles E. Bouchard, 'Journey of Faith: Initial Religious Formation as an Extension of the New Rite of Initiation of Adults', *Review for Religious*, 36:4 (1977), 592-599.

21. Eugene Duffy, 'Seminary Formation', *The Furrow*, 40:8 (1989), 451-460.

22. Donal Dorr, 'Forming Clergy and Laity Together', *The Furrow*, 41:11 (1990), 633.

23. Ibid., 635.

24. For one of the innumerable discussions of rites of initiation and rites of passage, see Mircea Eliade, *Rites and Symbols of Initiation*, New York: Harper and Row, 1958, esp. p. x.

25. A footnote in the American edition of *Lumen Gentium* (*Documents of Vatican* II) suggests this role of community over against the individual as such: 'The sacraments are here envisaged not as the actions of individuals but in their relation to the entire Church, whose life they articulate.' (footnote 33, p. 27 of Walter M. Abbott (ed.), *Documents of Vatican II*, New York: American Press, 1966).

26. The thought of the minister merely initiating the sacraments sounds so scandalous perhaps because we have paid little attention to the efficacy of initiating and its relationship with ritual. Admitting that the sacraments are not magic, we are not sure how to describe completely the efficacy of the actual event. Much help regarding this question may be found in the studies of Mary Douglas, *Purity and Danger*, and *Natural Symbols*, New York: Random House, 1970, and also in Herbert Fingarette's *Confucius: The Secular as Sacred*, New York: Harper and Row, 1972.

27. See Charles E. Bouchard, 'Journey of faith: Initial Religious Formation as an Extension of the New Rite of Initiation of Adults' in *Review for Religious*, 36:4 (1977), 592-599 and also Eugene Duffy, 'Seminary Formation' in *The Furrow* 40:8 (1989), 451-460. In these two articles the idea of using the new rite of initiation of adults as a model for formation of religious is renewed and re-introduced.

28. The literature to support this claim is abundant. Perhaps the best single collection is found in Seán Mac Réamoinn, (ed.), *Pobal: The Laity in the Church*, Dublin: Columba Pess, 1986.

Glossary

Religious Studies
Religious studies is the study of the phenomena of religion. The teacher seeks to present the religious topic with objectivity and impartiality. Buddhism, Judaism, Hinduism, Islam, Christianity are examined as important influences in the human story for enlightenment and the search for ultimate meaning. Each country has its own native religions as an object of study. The intention of teaching religious studies is not normally to convince the students about the superiority of one particular faith over another but rather to discover the wisdoms of each religious tradition and to nurture the values of tolerance and respect.

Religious studies may be part of a school curriculum, especially in schools where a large number of religious beliefs exist among students. Religious studies may also be studied in a school with a particular religious identity.

Evangelisation
Evangelisation refers to the proclamation of the gospel. Evangelisation influences people to hear the Good News and to be open to God's word. Jesus commissioned his disciples to go out and announce the news of salvation to all. Evangelisation is an essential element in the mission of the Church. Mark's gospel states: 'Jesus went into Galilee. There he proclaimed the gospel from God saying "The time is fulfilled and the kingdom of God is close at hand. Repent and believe the gospel"' (Mk 1:14-15). The *kerygma* is this proclamation. Evangelisation is usually directed to people who are without the Christian faith.

Catechesis
Catechesis follows evangelisation. Catechesis is concerned with the development of the Christian faith among believers. It is an exchange between believers. The word 'catechesis' is derived from a Greek word meaning to 'echo' because, after the second century, catechesis was aligned to the act of giving oral instruc-

tion to intending believers in the catechumenate. Catechesis seeks to foster faith, not just through learning doctrines but though the religious socialisation of the Christian community. Catechesis is an activity for believers and assumes that the participants have chosen to be present (or at least are willingly present) and are people of faith. Liturgy and engagement in good works are integral to catechesis.

The following are the chief goals of catechesis:
* to develop a sense of personal worth for each person created in the image of God.
* to empower people to live with values which are derived from the ethical stance of Christ.
* to assist in the celebration of life situations and liturgy, especially the eucharist.
* to initiate members of the Christian community into the stories and wisdoms of the Christian faith.
* to raise a consciousness of, and provide opportunities for, the realisation of the kingdom of God through a just society.
* to nurture the gift of imagination for the kingdom of God.
* to become attuned to the beauty and mystery of creation.
* to respond more actively to service of the poor.
* to be open to search for truth through an exploration of God's revelation in the world.
* to participate in the sacamental and prayerful life of the Church.
* to be more attuned in listening to God's word spoken through the bible, the teaching Church and the voices of the world in the cultural environment.
* to be recalled to a sense of sacred story in one's life journey and the life journeys of others.
* to grow in reconciliation through the transformation of failure and cross.
* to rejoice in the Good News of Christ and share the gospel through evangelisation and witness.

Religious Education
Religious education describes a relationship between religion and education. Religion is concerned with humankind's encounter with the divine. Religion helps people discover answers to such questions as 'What does life mean?' 'What is suffering?' 'Who is God?' Education is the endeavour to acquire knowledge, skills and values for the enhancement of human wisdoms. Education is a process of drawing out inherent gifts within individuals as well

as the transmission of knowledge, values and skills. Since the 19th century education has been closely linked with schooling but obviously education is much broader in its scope than a school system.

Religious education is the effort to know and experience the world of religion. Religious education does not mean leading a child or adult to a faith commitment but it may contribute to a position of faith affiliation. Religious education implies a conversation between learning and the whole experience of the phenomena of religion. Religious education may have all or some of the following features:

* Religious education is ongoing. It is not merely the transmission of knowledge.
* Religious education implies a dialogue between teacher and students.
* The content of religious education embraces the wisdoms of the religious heritage of world religions.
* Religious education may be considered from the perspective of religious studies or it may be of a confessional nature e.g. Religious education in the Catholic tradition or Christian religious education.
* The styles of religious education reflect the educational philosophy of the particular religion teacher.
* Social sciences, theology and scripture have a particular relevance to religious education.

Indoctrination
This word describes a style of religious teaching which does not permit deviation from the 'party line' and the official Church position. Indoctrination is intolerant of freedom of choice. No critical thought is permitted and religious development is channelled into prescribed boundaries. Indoctrination cultivates a hostile view towards other groups as threats to its ideology. Truth is what the teacher says is true. Indoctrination is contrary to the spirit of Jesus who invited people to stay about in a free choice situation: 'Come and see' (Jn 1:39).

Adult Religious Education
Adult religious education is faith education for adults on the life journey. Adult education focuses on participants who are adults and hence needs to be faithful to principles of adult learning. Adults bring to each learning situation a wealth of faith and life experiences and expect some opportunity for dialogue and shar-

ing of insights as partners in learning. Relevance is a basic principle for adult faith education. Busy adults have little time or energy for engaging in esoteric pursuits of remote academic questions. The term 'longlife' religious education might be more helpful than adult religious education because it suggests a gradual evolution of learning passages rather than a clear differentiation between child and adult learning.

Christian Doctrine
Christian doctrine relates to the learning of dogma. Christian doctrine concentrates on the acquisition of knowledge of doctrines. It is an enterprise of the mind rather than the heart. The term 'Christian Instruction' is similar to Christian Doctrine and emphasises a cognitive approach to learning about a particular faith tradition.

Christian Living
'Christian Living' was a popular term for Christian religious education during the 1970s. The term focused on the experiential dimension of Christian religious education, rather than the dogmatic or intellectual bias of Christian doctrine approaches. Christian living usually has a community involvement. The practical and real aspects of Christian living sought to appeal to students who were disillusioned with the aridity of the catechism. 'Christian Living' lessons were not normally concerned with philosophical questions but rather with the application of Christian teachings to ordinary life. One of the limits of this approach was the paucity of content in many of the lessons where students felt they had discussed to death how they felt about friendship, drugs etc. but knew little or nothing about the magnificant heritage of the Christian story and other religious traditions.

Christian Religious Education (often shortened to *Christian Education*)

Christian religious education is religious educaion which is explicitly Christian in its focus. Christian religious education situates its religious education firmly within the the Jesus story and the values of the Christian community. Within the concept of Christian religious education various churches have their own specific traditions. For example, Catholic religious education would have some specific dimensions, such as the doctrine of the communion of saints, which have a particular meaning within this tradition. However, in the contemporary ecumenical climate and dialogue most themes in Christian religious education are common to the educational endeavours of the mainline Christian Churches.

Select Bibliography

Abbott, W. M. (ed.), *The Documents of Vatican II*, London: Geoffrey Chapman, 1966.

Adult Education Commission Working Party. *Adults and Education: A Survey 1982-83*. Dublin: Government Publications, 1983.

Alberigo, Giuseppe/Provost, James (Eds.), 'Synod 1985: An Evaluation', *Concilium* 188:6 (1986).

Ball, Peter. *Adult Believing: A Guide to the Christian Initiation of Adults*, London: Mowbray, 1988.

Baum, Gregory. *Commentary on the Constitution of the Church of Vatican II*. New York: Deus Books / Paulist Press, 1967.

Bausch, William J. 'The role of the Sacraments in the Formation of Faith', *Living Light*, 14 (1977), 294-311.

Beaudoin, David M. 'A Personalist Approach to Catechesis', *Worship* 62 (1988), 237-249.

Beraudy, Roger. 'The New Ritual for Adult Baptism', *Theology Digest* 24:1 (1976), 57-62.

Bishops' Conference of England and Wales. Commission conducted by Kevin Nichols, *Guidelines for Religious Education 1: Cornerstone*, Slough: St. Paul Publications, 1978.

Blazquez, Ricardo. *Neo-Catechumenal Communities: A Theological Discernment*, Trans: Peter Corbishley, Slough: St Paul Publications, 1988.

Bouchard, Charles E. 'Journey of Faith: Initial Religious Formation as an extension of the New Rite of Initiation of Adults', *Review for Religious* 36:4 (1977), 592-599.

Boucher, Peter. *Adult Religious Education - How? Needs, Objectives and Methods*. An M.A. dissertation submitted to the University of Ulster at Magee College, 1987.

Boucher, Peter. 'Adult Religious Education', *Intercom*, November, 1990, 12-13.

Bourgeois, Henri. *On Becoming Christian: Christian Initiation and its*

Sacraments, Mystic, Connecticut: Twenty-third Publications, 1984.

Brady, Ray. 'Will our Children Believe and Belong?', *The Furrow*, 41:1 (1990), 3-8.

Brennan, Padraic. *Power in Rite: Celebrating R.C.I.A.* (RCIA U.K. Library 3) London: T. Shand Publications, 1986.

Breslin, Ann. *A Survey of Religious, Moral and Civic Values of Senior School-goers*. Maynooth: Research and Development Unit, 1983.

Breslin, Ann./Weafer, John. *Religious Beliefs, Practice and Moral Attitudes: A Comparison of Two Irish Surveys*. Maynooth: Council for Research and Development, 1985.

Buckley, Francis J. 'A Report on the 1977 Synod on Catechesis', *Lumen Vitae*, 32 (1977), 497-501.

Burghardt, W. 'Catechesis in the Early Chuch', *The Living Light* 1 (1964), 110-118.

Carey, Liam. 'Adult Religious Education', *The Irish Catechist*, 1 (1977), 48-57.

Casey, Nichols A. 'Short Ladder to Nowhere – The Crisis in Senior Religion', *The Furrow*, 35:2 (1984), 103 - 108.

Catechetical Association of Ireland. 'C.A.I. Survey on Religion. Religious Studies as a Subject for Leaving Certificate', *Irish Catechist*, 2:1 (1978), 14-23.

Charytanski, Ian/Lebeau, Paul. 'The Fifth Synod of Bishops and the Church's Catechetical Mission', *Lumen Vitae*, 33 (1978), 19-35.

Coget, Marcel. 'Cathechesis in a Christian Community. The formation of 12 to 13 year-old school children', *Lumen Vitae*, 24:4 (1972), 624-638.

Collins, Mary. *Contemplative Participation: Sacrosanctum Concilium Twenty Years Later*. Dublin: Columba Press, 1990.

Commission of Pope Paul VI. 'Sources of Catechesis and their Use', *Living Light*, 6 (1969), 6-34.

Commission on Adult Education. *Lifelong Learning - Report of the Commission on Adult Education*. Dublin: Stationary Office, 1983.

Congregation for Catholic Education. *The Religious Dimension of Education in a Catholic School*. Rome: Vatican Press, 1988.

Connolly, Declan. 'St Lucy's R.C.I.A. in Praxis', *The Irish Catechist*, 7:4 (1983), 9-16.

Convey, Martin A. *Adult Catechesis and Vatican II: Historical Roots and Irish Post-Conciliar Perspectives*. A dissertation submitted to the National University for the degree of Ph.D., 1992.

Cooney, Tom. 'Parish Cells', *Intercom*, December 1990/January 1991, 14 - 15.

Daly, Gabriel. 'The Church: Community of Faith' *The Furrow* 34:1 (1983), 403-414.

De Boy, James J. Jr. *Getting Started in Adult Religious Education*, New York: Paulist Press, 1979.

Devitt, Patrick M. *How Adult is Adult Religious Education? Gabriel Moran's Contribution to Adult Religious Education*, Dublin: Veritas, 1991.

Devitt, Patrick M. 'The Educational Debate: Faith and Education in Dialogue', *Doctrine and Life* 42:3 (1992), 115-123.

Devitt, Patrick M. *That You May Believe: A Brief History of Religious Eduction*. Dublin: Dominican Publications, 1992.

Directory of Adult Religious Education in Ireland. Dublin: Veritas, 1985.

Documents of the Fifth Synod of Bishops, Rome 1977. Dublin: Veritas Publications, 1977.

Dorr, Donal. 'Forming Clergy and Laity Together', *The Furrow*, 41:11 (1990), 632 - 638.

Duffy, Regis A. *On Becoming a Catholic: The Challenge of Christian Initiation*. London: Harper & Row, 1984.

Duggan, Robert. 'Implementing the Rite of Christian Initiation of Adults', *Living Light* 17:4 (1980), 327-333.

Dujarier, Michel. *The Rites of Christian Initiation - Historical and Pastoral Reflections*, trans. Kevin Hart, New York: Sadlier, 1979.

Dulles, Avery. *Models of the Church*. Dublin: 1976.

Dunning, James B. 'The Rite of Christian Initiation of Adults: Model of Church Growth', *Worship* 53 (1979), 142-156.

Dunning, James B., *Ministries – Sharing God's Gifts*, Winona, Minnesota: Saint Mary's Press, 1985.

Dunning, James B. *New Wine, New Wineskins: Exploring the R.C.I.A.*, New York: Sadlier, 1981.

Erdozain, Luis. 'The Evolution of catechetics - A Survey of Six International Study Weeks on Catechetics', *Lumen Vitae* 25 (1970), 7-31.

Figgess, Sandra. *Christian Initiation of Older Children*, Slough: St Paul Publications, 1990.

Flannery, Austin (ed.). *Vatican Council II: the Conciliar and Post Conciliar Documents*, Dublin: Dominican Publications, 1981.

Flannery, Austin (ed.). *Vatican Council II: More Post Conciliar Documents*, Dublin: Dominican Publications, 1982.

Flannery, Tony. 'Religious in Decline - articulating the pain', *The Furrow* 43: 1 (1992), 32-35.

Fleming, Ted (ed.) *Directory of Adult Religious Education in Ireland*, Dublin: Veritas, 1985.

Gallagher, Michael Paul. 'Atheism Irish Style', *The Furrow* 25 (1974), 183-192.

Gallagher, Michael Paul. 'What Hope for Irish Faith'. *The Furrow*, 1978.

Gallagher, Michael Paul. *Help My Unbelief*. Dublin: Veritas, 1983.

Gallagher, Michael Paul. *Free To Believe: Ten Steps To Faith*, London: Darton, Longman and Todd, 1987.

Gallagher, Michael Paul. *Struggles of Faith*, Dublin: The Columba Press, 1990.

Gallagher, Michael Paul. 'Faith and Our New Culture', *The Furrow* 41:6 (1990), 347 - 352.

Gobbel, Roger A. 'Christian Education with Adolescents: An Invitation to Thinking', *Living Light*, 17 (1980), 134-143.

Greinacher, Norbert/Elizondo, Virgil (Edts.) 'Religion in the Eighties', *Concilium* 174 (1984).

Groome, Thomas H. *Christian Religious Education - sharing our story and vision*, New York: Harper & Row, 1981.

Gurrieri, John A. 'The New Language of Christian Initiation', *Liturgy* 4:1 (1983), 16-17.

Hanna, Tony. 'The Catholic Youth - An Endangered Species', *The Furrow* 38:2 (1987).

Healy, Sean J./Reynolds Brigid. (on behalf of the Conference of Major Religious Superiors [Ireland]). *Ireland Today - Reflecting in the Light of the Gospel* . Dublin: Justice Office, 1985.

Healy, Sean/Reynolds, Brigid. *Irish Society and The Future of Education*, Dublin: Irish Messenger Publications, 1986.

Hixon, Barbara. *RCIA Ministry – an Adventure into Mayhem and Mystery*, San Jose, California: Resource Publications Inc., 1989.

Hogan, Mary. 'Keeping the faith', *The Furrow* 34:3 (1983), 135-144.

Hull, John. (ed.), *New Directions in Religious Education*, Sussex: The Falmer Press, 1982

Inglis, Thomas. *How Religious are Irish University Students?* Maynooth: Research and Development Unit Report, 1979.

Irish Episcopal Commission for Catechetics. *A Syllabus for Religious Education of Pupils in Post-Primary Schools*. Dublin: Veritas, 1982.

Irish Episcopal Conference, *Handing on the Faith in the Home*, Dublin: Veritas, 1980.

Ivory, Thomas P. 'The Restoration of the Catechumenate as a Norm for Catechesis', *Living Light* 13:2 (1976), 225-235.

Ivory, Thomas P. *Conversion and Community - A Catechumenal Model for total Parish Formation*, New York: Paulist Press, 1988.

Joyce, Margaret Mary. 'Becoming a Christian Today', *The Irish Catechist*, 7:3 (1983), 25-27.

Kavanagh, Aidan. 'The Norm of Baptism: The Rite of Christian Initiation of Adults', *Worship*, 48:3 (1974), 143-152.

Kemp, Raymond B. *A Journey in Faith - An Experience of the Catechumenate*. New York: Sadlier, 1979.

Kirby, Peadar. *Is Irish Catholicism Dying?*, Dublin: Mercier Press, 1984.

Kretschmar, Georg. 'Recent Research on Christian Initiation', *Studia Liturgica* 12: 2/3 (1977), 87-106.

Lacey, Liam. 'Adult Catechesis in Ireland: A Way Forward', *The Irish Catechist*, 7:3 (1983), 31-41.

Lane, Dermot A. (ed.), *Religious Education and the Future - Essays in Honour of Patrick Wallace*, Dublin: Columba Press, 1986.

Lane, Dermot A. *Catholic Education and the School: Some theological reflections*. Dublin: Veritas, 1991.

Lane, Dermot A. (ed.), *Religion, Education and the Constitution*. Dublin: Columba Press, 1992.

MacGréil, Micheál. 'Church attendance and religious practice of Dublin Adults', *Social Studies* 3:2 (1974), 163-211.

MacGréil, Micheál. *Educational Participation in Ireland*. A Report published by the Survey and Research Unit, Department of Social Studies, St. Patrick's College, Maynooth, Co. Kildare, February 1990.

MacGréil, Micheál. *Religious Practice and Attitudes in Ireland: A Survey of Religious Attitudes and Practice and Related Issues in the Republic of Ireland 1988-1989*. A Report published by the Survey and Research Unit, Department of Social Studies, St. Patrick's College, Maynooth, Co. Kildare. March, 1991.

Mac Mahon, Bernadette. *A Study of Religion among Catholic Adolescents Attending some Dublin Schools*, Maynooth: Research and Development Unit, 1981.

MacRéamoinn, Seán (ed.). *Pobal: The Laity in the Church*. Dublin: Columba Press, 1986.

McCann, Joseph. 'Adult Religious Education - why a faith community is not yet being built', *The Irish Catechist*, 7:4 (1983), 4-8.

McNamara, Kevin. *Curriculum and Values in Education*, Dublin: Veritas, 1987.

Mongove, Anne Marie. 'Catechesis and Liturgy', *Worship*, 61 (1987), 248-259.

Moran, Gabriel. *Vision and Tactics: Towards an Adult Church* London: Burns & Oates, 1968.

Moran, Gabriel. *God Still Speaks: The Basis of Christian Education*. London: Search Press, 1970.

Moran, Gabriel. *Education Toward Adulthood*, Dublin: Gill and Macmillan, 1980.

Moriarty, Marian. 'Post Primary R.E.', *The Irish Catechist*, 1 (Winter 1977), 17-20.

Mulcahy, D.G./O' Sullivan, Denis (eds.) *Irish Educational Policy: Process and Substance*. Dublin: Institute of Public Administration, 1989.

Murphy Center for Liturgical Research. *Made, not Born: New Perspectives on Christian Initiation and the Catechumenate*, Notre Dame: University of Notre Dame Press, 1980.

Murphy, Con. *Adult Education in Ireland*. Dublin: Stationary Office, 1973.

✠ Murphy, Michael. *The Parish: The Challenge Ahead*. Cork: The Printing House, 1986.

Murphy, Michael W. 'The maturing Status of Adult Education', *Reality* 39:2 (1975), 44-46.

✠ Murray, Donal. 'The Roman Synod', *Irish Catechist*, 1:3 (1977), 27-29.

✠ Murray, Donal. *Youth in the Church: A Shared Challenge*, Dublin: Veritas, 1985.

✠ Murray, Donal. *A Special Concern - The Philosophy of Education: a Christian Perspective*, Dublin: Veritas, 1991.

Murtagh, Desmond. 'Will our Children Have Faith?', *The Furrow* 42:4 (1991), 221 - 226.

Myers, Gordon J./Whitehead, James/Whitehead, Evelyn. 'The Parish and Sacraments of Adulthood', *Listening* 12 (1977), 83 - 100.

NicGhiolla Phádraig, Máire. 'Religion in Ireland, Preliminary Analysis', *Social Studies* 5:2 (1976), 113-180.

NicGhiolla Phádraig, Máire. *A Survey of Religious Attitudes and Beliefs 1973-1974*. A dissertation submitted to U.C.D. for the degree of Ph.D., 1981.

NicGhiolla Phádraig, Máire. 'Trends in Religious Practice in Ireland', *Doctrine and Life* 42:11 (1992), 3-11.

O'Connor, Fergal. 'Religion in Irish Universities', *Doctrine and Life*, 17 (1967), 186-191.

O'Hare, Briege, 'Parish Catechesis', *Irish Catechist*, 5:3 (1981), 11-15.

O'Reilly, Sile. 'The Parish Catechist', *Intercom*, July/August, 1990, 12-14.

Parent, Reni. *A Church of the baptised - Overcoming the tension between the Clergy and Laity*. New York: Paulist Press, 1989.

Quinlan, Brendan. 'Adult Catechesis in the Parish', *Irish Catechist*, 8:2 (1984), 19-23.

Reichert, Richard. 'A Catechist's response to the RCIA', *Living Light* 14 (1977), 138-146.

Research and Development Unit, Catholic Communications Institute of Ireland. 'Survey of Catholic Clergy and Religious Personnel 1971', *Social Studies* 1 (1972), 137-234.

Reynolds, Brigid/Healy, Seán J. *Social Analysis in the Light of the Gospel*. Dublin: Justice Office, 1983.

Reynolds, Brigid/Healy, Seán. *Irish Society and the Future of Education*, Dublin: Irish Messenger Publications, 1986.

Rouine, Sr. Benedict. 'The Futue of Adult Religious Education', *Irish Catechist*, 8:3 (1984), 43-47.

Rouine, Sr. Benedict. 'Adult Religious Education', *Intercom*, February 1990, 15 - 16.

Ryan, Liam. 'Faith Under Survey', *The Furrow* 34:1 (1983), 3-15.

Saris, Wim. *Towards a Living Church - Family and Community Catechesis*, London: Collins, 1980.

Schillebeecks, Edward. *The Church with a Human Face: A New Expanded Theology of Ministry*, London: 1985.

Schillebeecks, Edward. *Ministry, a Case for Change*. London: 1985.

Sloyan, Virginia. 'The Liturgical Dimension of Catechesis', *American Ecclesiastical Review*, 160 (1968), 255-261.

Tavard, G.H., *A Theology for Ministry*. Wilmington, Delaware: 1983.

Tierney, Philip. 'Senior Cycle R.E.', *The Irish Catechist* 5:4 (1981), 23-27.

Upton, Julia. *A Church for the Next Generation - Sacraments in Transition*, Collegeville, Minnesota: The Liturgical Press, 1990.

Verheecke, Marie-Adele. 'Parish Catechesis Today', *Lumen Vitae* 42:3 (1987), 324-328.

Walsh, Kathleen. 'Questioning the Idea of 'Lay Ministries', *New Blackfriars* 68 (1987), 504-515.

Walsh, Margaret. 'The Education Debate: The Future of Catholic Secondary Schools', *Doctrine and Life* 42:4 (1992), 171-180.

Warren, Michael (ed.). *Source Book for Modern Catechetics*, Minnesota: St Mary's Press, 1983.

Warren, Michael. *Faith, Culture and the Worshipping Community - Shaping the Practice of the Local Church*, New York: Paulist Press, 1989.

Weafer, John A. 'Vocations - A Review of National and International Trends', *The Furrow* 31 (1988), 501-511.

Weafer, John A./Hanley, Ann M. *Whither Religious Education? A Survey of Post-Primary Teachers in Ireland with Commentaries edited by Dermot A. Lane*. Dublin: The Columba Press, 1991.

Westerhoff, John H. III. *Will Our Children Have Faith*, New York: Seabury Press, 1976.

Westerhoff, John H. III./Edwards, O.C. Jnr. *A Faithful Church: Issues in the History of Catechesis*, Wilton, Connecticut: Morehouse-Barlow Co. Inc., 1981.

Westerhoff, John H. III. 'Liturgics and Catechetics', *Worship* 61 (1987), 510-516.

White, James W. 'In Process: A Theology for Adult Christian Education', *Lumen Vitae*, 37 (1982), 413-430.

Wörgul, George S. 'The Ecclesiology of the Rite of Christian Initiation of Adults', *Louvain Studies* 6:2 (1976), 159-169.